# FROM DREAM TO REALITY

## 7 STEPS TO SETTING UP A SMALL BUSINESS

Pavlenka Small

authorHOUSE®

AuthorHouse™
1663 Liberty Drive
Bloomington, IN 47403
www.authorhouse.com
Phone: 1-800-839-8640

First published by AuthorHouse   2/24/2011

ISBN: 978-1-4567-7507-0 (sc)

Printed in the United States of America

Any people depicted in stock imagery provided by Thinkstock are models, and such images are being used for illustrative purposes only.
Certain stock imagery © Thinkstock.

This book is printed on acid-free paper.

## DEDICATION

To Lauren Jeffs, a budding young entrepreneur
who was the inspiration to write this book

# Contents

# Introduction

*'Everyone has a talent. What is rare is the courage to follow the talent to the dark place where it leads.'*

**Erica Jong**

Starting up your own business is an exciting prospect but it can also be a daunting one. This user-friendly, no-nonsense guide to setting up your own business aims to inform you and point you in the right direction. It will allow you to carefully consider if you have what it takes to successfully set up and run your own business and join the growing ranks of the self-employed.

Many people never fulfil a deep-rooted desire to become their own boss for fear of failure and often spend many years in a job or career that they find totally unfulfilling, remaining employed because it is a 'safer' option.

It is not enough to simply have a good idea and hope to make a living out of it. There are currently 4 million businesses operating in the UK but sadly 83% of all new start-up businesses fail within the first year and 80% of all new businesses fail within the first 3-5 years. If you don't run your business well, it could fail within 5 years.( ref:-Small Business Administration)

Covering all aspects of what you need to know and consider as a prospective business owner, 'Small Steps To Setting Up Your Own Small Business' gives you informative, honest and practical advice, as well as useful activities and action points in 7, easy to follow STEPS.

So don't become another unsuccessful statistic. Read this guide, do your planning and I wish you well with you exciting new business venture.

Good Luck!

Pavlenka Small

# STEP 1
## Do you have what it takes to be your own boss?

This first step looks at you: your qualities, skills and capabilities as well as identifying any skills you may have or training needs in order to fully equip you to set up and run your own business.

> *'Choose a job you love and you will never
> have to work a day in your life.'*

> **Confucius**

## All about you—you ARE the business

It is one thing to have a good idea for a business but quite another to make a successful business out of your idea. Most employed people take their weekly or monthly salary for granted, but once you enter the realms of self-employment, this becomes an unknown quantity.

The reality of your dream business will invariably mean that you work extremely long hours without much, or indeed any, immediate financial gain. Add into the equation the fact you suddenly find yourself responsible for new and different tasks and skills, it can begin to make the idea of setting up on one's own seem less appealing.

It is also important to be mindful of the fact that being self-employed is just a business and not a life-style and for that reason, it is crucial you do not lose sight of maintaining a work/life balance which not only suits you, but your nearest and dearest as well.

However, do not be disheartened, it is not all doom and gloom! Just as success in business does not happen by chance and you will be expected to work hard, cope with some knocks along the way and at times, push yourself outside your comfort zone, the rewards of being self-employed CAN undoubtedly outweigh the world of working for someone else.

Consider for a moment, anything you have had to work hard for in your life. Perhaps the qualifications you gained at college, university or work. It may have been tough at times, but how did you benefit from your hard work and determination, long-term?

Setting up a business is no different and, as with anything in life, a certain attitude and approach can go a very long way to achieving the desired outcomes.

Top entrepreneur, Peter Jones, of Dragon's Den fame, has some tips for making a business a success:-

- **Have vision-** otherwise you won't know where you are heading
- **Market yourself-**through business competitions and other networking events
- **Confidence-** believe in yourself and your idea
- **Commitment-**to a common goal
- **Aim for results-**planning is the key
- **Take action—**to get from where you are now to where you want to be
- **Timing-**anticipating the changing market is crucial
- **Perseverance-** successful entrepreneurs battle against the odds
- **Be caring—**relationships with people are the key
- **Inituition-** use it to help make the right decisions

Smallsteps2success personal development and career coaching suggests the following **PRODUCE** model as being essential components to consider when successfully setting up and maintaining a new business:-

**P**lanning
**R**esearch
**O**rganisation
**D**etermination
**U**-(You are the key to success!)
**C**hange
**E**nthusiasm

**When the going gets tough—the self-employed hang on in there!**

You will find being self-employed will present different challenges and most of how you view your ventures' progress and success (or otherwise), will be determined by your perceptions, beliefs and thoughts. Remember, anything that is worth having needs to be worked at and just as you will have been faced with unexpected challenges as an employee, so to will you experience set-backs as a new business owner

How good are you at thinking 'outside the box'? Can you draw on your innermost resourcefulness when faced with difficult situations and decision making? If not, who can you contact who will offer appropriate help and advice? There are always people on hand to help you through even the most difficult of times. (See step 7-useful contacts).

**Mistakes? What mistakes? Look on them as learning opportunities!**

When things don't go according to plan, try not to see

them as unmitigated disasters but rather as an opportunity to learn. Consider all the well-known phrases such as: 'it's easy to be wise after the event,' and 'if only I'd seen that coming'. These and similar sayings will come into your mind on more than one occasion. Look on your journey as a huge learning curve and be prepared for a bit of a roller coaster ride. Henry Ford once said: 'even a mistake may turn out to be the one thing necessary to a worthwhile achievement.' Where would we be today without our motor cars? Thomas Edison declared: 'I have not failed. I've just found 10,000 ways that won't work,' when he created the first working light bulb.

Consider that YOU and only YOU are in control of your own destiny, (admittedly, perhaps just to a certain extent), and therefore, if something has not gone according to plan, consider what went wrong and why, re-focus and decide how to **react** to it and **act** on it in a positive and constructive way.

You will be surprised how, at times, your energy and enthusiasm will know no boundaries and even though you may be working towards something business related most of your waking day, it will be **your** responsibility and you **will** hold the key to your success.

### Woman/man or machine? You cannot do it all!

Many new start-up business owners make the mistake of believing they need to do everything themselves, more often than not to save themselves money. However, what can often be saved in monetary terms can often take up your valuable time and, as a consequence, you end up not running your business efficiently and professionally.

It is great if you are good with technology and want to devise your own website, but if, like many people you fear what you need to do in order to produce the end results, why not invest in a professional web designer, (who is the specialist in their field), thus freeing up your valuable time to concentrate on what you **are** good at. It is your business, after all, so why involve yourself in aspects you don't enjoy that could be achieved more successfully and professionally in half the time, by an expert?

## ACTIVITY 1…
### BIDE YOUR TIME EXERCISE

This activity is to examine whether you have what it takes to be your own boss. Allow yourself some time on your own where you will not be disturbed and focus on yourself rather than your business. It is important that you are honest with yourself as well!

If you agree with the sentence, award yourself 3 marks per sentence, 1 mark if you disagree and 2 if you are unsure one way or the other.

| Beliefs | Marks |
| --- | --- |
| I am open to new ideas | _____ |
| When something works well for me, I do more of the same | _____ |
| When something isn't working, I change it | _____ |
| I believe strongly in my own abilities | _____ |
| I believe strongly in the abilities of others | _____ |
| I am happy to ask for help if there are gaps in my knowledge | _____ |
| Delegation is important to me and my staffs' development | _____ |
| I can resolve problems or disputes easily and amicably | _____ |
| I can hold my own ground when right, without upsetting others | _____ |
| I am prepared to do whatever I ask my staff to do, myself | _____ |
| I do it now and don't procrastinate | _____ |
| I set goals with a flexible approach, changing them as circumstances require | _____ |
| TOTAL: | _____ |

(MAXIMUM MARKS = 36)

| **I** - YOUR PERSONALITY | **Marks** |
|---|---|
| I am enthusiastic | _____ |
| I have a positive attitude | _____ |
| I relate to people well | _____ |
| I am organised | _____ |
| I am good at setting priorities | _____ |
| I am non-judgemental | _____ |
| I am honest | _____ |
| I am ethical | _____ |
| I admit my mistakes | _____ |
| I give reasons rather than excuses | _____ |
| I value my abilities | _____ |
| I am ready, willing and able to improve myself | _____ |
| I am even-tempered | _____ |
| I can look at things objectively | _____ |
| I accept constructive criticism | _____ |
| I am fair | _____ |
| I give praise where it is due | _____ |
| I practice what I preach | _____ |
| TOTAL: | _____ |

(MAXIMUM MARKS = 54)

| Determination | Marks |
|---|---|
| I am totally committed to my personal success | _____ |
| I am totally committed to the success of my business | _____ |
| I am totally committed to supporting my staff | _____ |
| I am committed to continually striving to improve my business | _____ |
| I will pay my debts on time | _____ |
| I will be punctual for appointments | _____ |
| I will always 'go the extra mile' | _____ |
| I will do whatever it takes to grow my business | _____ |
| TOTAL: | _____ |

(MAXIMUM MARKS = 24)

| Excellence | Marks |
| --- | --- |
| I have a good business idea | _____ |
| I will honour my promises and guarantees | _____ |
| I can be relied upon | _____ |
| I will strive to under-promise and over-deliver | _____ |
| I will always do the best I can in any given situation | _____ |
| I believe only the best is good enough for my clients | _____ |
| I believe only the best is good enough for me | _____ |
| TOTAL: | _____ |

(MAXIMUM MARKS = 21)

## TOTAL MARKS OUT OF 135:      _____

If you have scored less than half the possible marks for each section of this exercise you will need to consider what you need to change or improve upon in order to be more equipped to successfully make a go of being your own boss.

## Your vision

Whilst it is one thing to have a good business idea, (which you are undoubtedly passionate about), it is quite another story when considering whether or not you can make a living out of your business idea. Many new business owners make the mistake of transferring their old employee mindset; having a job or career is not the same thing as setting up, developing, monitoring and altering your business as internal and external circumstances dictate. Different attitudes, goals and methods of working will undoubtedly have to be developed and acquired. And don't forget, just as this is 'your baby', once you employ staff, do not expect them to be as dedicated and passionate about your business as you are!

More of this in Stage 2 but do not be disheartened. If you have a sound business idea and follow the PRODUCE model, there is no reason why you cannot create a successful business.

# ACTIVITY 2 …
# YOUR BUSINESS VISION

This activity is the start to your planning process. Using the chart below, (which includes a couple of examples to help you get started), describe your business idea. What is it? Where will it be based? (At home,online or in a shop/office).

What will this give you? Merely disliking your current job is not a good enough reason to set up on your own. Will self-employment give you greater freedom and independence? Will it allow you to realise a life-long ambition? Perhaps it will enable you to work part-time rather than full-time or give you greater job satisfaction?

Now is the time to be honest about what it is you want to achieve and why. It is also important to consider the potential disadvantages as well as the advantages; try taking those rose- tinted spectacles off while you complete the following activity.

| My Business Vision | What My Business Will Give Me |
|---|---|
| A brief description of what you will be selling, to whom and where | eg - improved quality of life |

| My Strengths | My Weaknesses |
|---|---|
| • self-motivated<br><br>• willing to listen & learn | • I don't take criticism easily<br><br>• I find it hard to plan ahead and see the bigger picture |

Now consider what existing skills and abilities you have which will be useful to your business and what skills and qualifications you may need to acquire, in order to plug any gaps in your expertise.

# ACTIVITY 3 …
# YOUR SKILLS

This activity concentrates on the existing transferable skills you have developed with time and experience and which will be useful for your new business. Equally it allows you to consider what gaps there are in your knowledge and skills set, that you may have to develop for your new business venture.

| Existing Skills | Skills Required |
|---|---|
| | |
| | |
| | |
| | |

# STEP I ACTION POINTS:

◊   activity1--BIDE your time

◊   activity 2—What's your vision

◊   activity 3—skills analysis

# STEP 2
## Fail to plan, plan to fail

Essential planning and research needed
to build a successful business.

*'Good plans shape good decisions. That's why planning helps to make elusive dreams come true.'*

**Lester Robert Bittel**

Now that you have identified your existing skills and those that you might need to develop, it is time to start thinking about what strategies, processes, research and information you need to consider.

The biggest cause of failure for start ups are; setting your sights too high, not researching your market thoroughly, hiring the wrong staff and not putting enough funds aside for contingency. So it's important to keep your eye on these potential pitfalls.

However, a good starting point is to have a clearly defined plan of what your business is all about and what you need to do in order to make it all happen! It can be argued that there is no ideal order to complete the 7 Steps outlined in this book as long as you cover all that is necessary for your business. Look on the process as being a bit like completing a jigsaw puzzle; as long as you arrive at the finished picture, the way you slot in the individual pieces is not an issue. You will find that as you work on developing your business, things will have a way of falling naturally into place, so do not be too concerned as to what is the right or wrong way in which to complete various activities.

Step 1 allowed you to have a clear idea of what your business vision is and it is a good idea to begin with a start date. It is important to be aware that your actual start date will be determined by many variables including things that are often outside your personal control. Business launch dates are frequently delayed by issues such as not being able to get planning permission in time, banks taking their time to secure finance (if applicable) and delays in the delivery of supplies and furniture. Take heart and remember, you are hoping your business will operate for some time to come so whilst doing what you can to speed things up it may be a question of accepting that some delays are inevitable.

You will have a clearer idea of your ideal start date once you have considered all that you need to set into place, in order to be able to commence trading or offering your services.

So what are the things you need to consider as part of your initial planning process?

Setting goals are important as they give you something to focus on and work towards. They also allow you to visualise what your expected success will look like. Can you, for example, visualise what your office/shop/products/services will look like? Who will your ideal customer(s) be? What will you need to buy, rent, lease for your business to be fully functional? Without focused goals you may waste time pursuing things that are fun and exciting at the expense of things that are important to your business and its future success.

Without doubt you will be involved in something you are passionate about and, as you will be living and breathing your new business 24/7, energy and enthusiasm are musts in order to break through glass ceilings and break down doors. However, you also need to be aware of the importance of practical organisation and planning.

# ACTIVITY 1
# INITIAL PLANNING QUESTIONS TO CONSIDER

1. Does your idea suit your personality and will your idea work for you?

2. What do you want to get out of your business, both personally and professionally?

3. Do you have the skills and experience? (Refer back to STEP 1)

4. Does your business concept rely on your abilities and prior knowledge or will you need to 'buy in' experts?

5. Do you have the time commitment, energy and support to put things into practice?

6. Do you have the necessary contacts to help you start your proposed business?

7. Have you taken into account the resources you will need in terms of money, equipment and premises?

8. What competition do you expect to face?

9. Can it succeed in the market place?

10. Is there sufficient demand for your products/ services?

11. Will you be able to make a profit? If so, when?

12. Have you considered all your costs?

13. Will you set prices that the market will bear?

This list serves to start the thinking process required and you may think of other considerations. Now on to setting some planning goals!

## WHO WILL YOUR CUSTOMERS BE?

**Step 3** takes a look at all aspects of marketing but at this stage, it is wise to think about your 'market'. The market refers to the type of customers you want and hope to attract to your products and services.

There are several ways in which you can identify your ideal customers. You can ask friends, family and work colleagues what they would expect to pay for your product or services by devising a questionnaire. It is important that you ask relevant and appropriate questions in order to gather as much useful information as possible.

You may decide to act as a mystery shopper. This is another way of doing some market research by visiting similar businesses as a customer, to compare what is currently available in the field. Make sure you know what you are looking for before you visit. Take a list where you can identify the age and sex of the customers using the goods and services on offer and make a note of what is on sale and the price range.

You can also use the internet to find out what is currently available in similar businesses to yours. This can range from prices, how goods are packaged, variety of products and so on.

There are some sites which will give you an idea of the economics of your chosen area. Called social demographics, this is handy if, for example, you plan to open up a luxury designer dress shop and yet the town you have chosen has one of the highest figures of unemployment in the country!

# <u>ACTIVITY 2</u>
# <u>YOUR MARKET</u>

As a starting point, before you do much market research, answer the following questions as thoroughly as you can at this stage:

+ Who is your ideal customer(s)?—age, gender, socio-economic background. (Are they likely to shop in Lidl,Tesco or Waitrose?)

-------------------------------------------------------------------

-------------------------------------------------------------------

-------------------------------------------------------------------

-------------------------------------------------------------------

+ What price will these customers be prepared to pay for your product(s) and service(s)? (Are you aiming for the lower end of the market, the middle or the top end?). What is your pricing structure based on?

-------------------------------------------------------------------

-------------------------------------------------------------------

-------------------------------------------------------------------

-------------------------------------------------------------------

+ Who are you competitors, both locally and nationally?

-------------------------------------------------------------------

-------------------------------------------------------------------

-------------------------------------------------------------------

-------------------------------------------------------------------

    ✦    Is there a market for you product? You may have a good idea but those of you who watch the TV show, 'Dragons Den', will appreciate that it takes more than a good idea to run a successful business.

------------------------------------------------------------

------------------------------------------------------------

------------------------------------------------------------

------------------------------------------------------------

As you will see later in STEP 3, it is important that all components of your business fit together and convey the right message. If you are hoping to attract the upper end of the market, for example, it is important that all your merchandising—business stationery, packaging and decor in your shop—all send out the same message as to what you are offering your customers.

## LOCATION, LOCATION, LOCATION. WHERE WILL YOUR BUSINESS BE BASED?

A report undertaken by Enterprise Nation in 2007[*] on home businesses showed that 60% of new businesses were started from home. This accounted for 28% of UK employment with a combined turnover of 364 billion and is equal to over 1,400 new businesses each week.

Individual types of business will determine what premises you opt for. It is worth spending time considering the pros and cons of working from home or investing in premises, based on your type of business, your finances and personal preferences.

---

[*]    www.bytestart.co.uk/content/news/statistics

If you are planning to work from home you will need to consider what equipment and commodities you need to invest in and where you will be working from.

If you have a family, you will also need to plan how to fit your business activities around your domestic arrangements, particularly if you have young children and space is at a premium.

If you do not have a dedicated office space you will need to decide how to organise your working space during the day and whether it will fit in with or disrupt your family routines.

If you need to store stock for your business, will you have the space?

If your property is mortgaged, you will need to inform your mortgage provider that you intend working for home and this may well increase your monthly payments. (There are also various business insurances to consider--as covered in STEP 6- Rules and regulations).

These may seem fairly obvious but it is easy to overlook such practicalities in the early stages of setting up your business and they are vital aspects of your planning process.

Assuming you need premises to operate your business from, it is crucial that you give careful consideration to where you locate your business and how to undertake appropriate research. It is strongly advised that you seek legal and financial advice before you sign on the dotted line.

The choice of location for your business can be the making or breaking of its success. Many factors need to be taken into consideration; whilst a high street position will most certainly raise your profile and create awareness of the existence of your business, you will need to consider the viability of having to pay out higher rent and business rates. If you choose to set up in a less expensive, quieter area, you will need to think about whether you will attract your target audience and whether they will be able to physically find you and park nearby.

You will also have to decide whether you are going to rent, lease or even purchase the property.

Many new business owners fail to accurately estimate what it will cost them to secure suitable business premises. This is why it is advisable to compile a business plan. (See STEP 5). Even if you do not need to raise finance from an external source to fund your business, a business plan allows you to look at all aspects of your business objectively.

# ACTIVITY3—
# WHERE WILL YOUR BUSINESS BE LOCATED?

List your reasons and explanations for your choice of the following.

+ Where do you want your business to be located and why?

---
---
---
---
---

+ What size and type of building are you looking for?

---
---
---
---

+ Will you need to apply for planning permission? (This can often be a lengthy process and may delay your anticipated opening date)

---
---
---
---

- What legal implications do you need to consider? (For example, is the property a listed building? Are here likely to any restrictions imposed by the local council?)

---

---

---

---

- Will deliveries be able to easily access the premises?

---

---

---

---

- What existing services are there and what services might you need to acquire?

---

---

---

---

- Will you buy, lease or rent your premises and what is your rationale for doing so?

---

---

---

---

## YOUR BUSINESS NAME—WILL IT STAND OUT AND GIVE THE RIGHT IMPRESSION?

Choosing an appropriate name for your business can often prove to be quite a challenge and is something many people deliberate over for some time.

It is important that the name you choose relates meaningfully to your business. Remember, you want to attract the type of customers you most want to do business with, so a name that might hold some personal significance to you, may have no relevance at all to your prospective customers.

Trying to be too clever or subtle with your choice of name, (e.g. a play on words or a hidden meaning), can often detract from the message you are trying to convey about your business. So why not run your proposed business name by a few people whose opinions you value and trust.

Also, if you plan to have a website, how easily will your site be found and does the name convey the right image for your company.

Consider what you want your name to say about you and what you are offering; will it attract the type of customers you want or will it send out mixed messages? Stand alone titles and names do not necessarily translate into ideal domain names eg: Children's Laughter becomes childrenslaughter and Powergen Italia becomes Powergenitalia!

You may want to keep your name simple and opt to just use your name e.g. John Brown—Estate Agent. Or you may want to use a memorable name or phrase. Ex Simply Red band member, Chris Joyce, set up a café called' 'Love Saves The Day' because he has always had to love what he does but also because: 'when people phone and you answer the phone saying—'Love Saves The Day' you get all sorts of responses like 'Oh, does it?!'

Your business name may relate to your actual product or service. (For example my first business --Trenchers Sandwich Bar—was so-named as a Trencher, a flat unleavened piece of dry bread, was the earliest form of a sandwich and not, as many assume, named after Lord Sandwich!).

Whatever name you choose, consider your choice carefully, ask a few trusted people their opinion of your choice and think about how prospective customers will find you, either online (via Google searches) or in business directories, (e.g. The Yellow Pages).

**There's only one MacDonald's!"**

You will want your business name to be unique so you will need to check if your proposed name is already being used by someone else.

**Companies House** is the main source of such information and they will also advise as to what wordings are appropriate and permissible.

If you want to check how universally appropriate and acceptable your trading name is, enter your company name into a language translation site such as www.babelfish.yahoo.com. For example, 'Nova' means 'don't go' in Spanish, which is possibly not the best name for a new car!

If you want to prevent other traders from using your name or something similar, it is possible to protect a trading name by registering it with the **Trade Marks Registry** at **The Patent Office.** (Refer to STEP 7). However, Trade marking is a slow, expensive process and not to be entered into without due consideration.

If you are trading as a Limited Company, you should be aware that you are required by Law to register your business name and address with Companies House, who hold a record of every single Limited Company in the UK.

If you are planning to create your own website, you will need to ensure you can use your business name as a website name as well.

Check by logging onto any web hosting site and enter your chosen name followed by: .co.uk or .com or some other top level domain such as .net or .org.

You can also check if a domain name is available by logging onto www.123-reg.co.uk and then register your domain name with a reputable domain name supplier such as www.easily.co.uk.

Be aware that when you start working on your own behalf, you must register for Income Tax and National Insurance purposes with Her Majesties Revenue and Customs, within three months of trading www.hmrc.gov.uk takes you through the required process.

### What will your business structure be?

Before you talk to the bank, solicitor or accountant, you will need to think about what structure you will operate within. Do you intent setting up as a sole trader, a partnership or a limited company?

95% of the nearly 430 million small businesses registered in the UK are either Sole Traders, single-director companies, partnerships or self-employed owner-managers employing less than 5 people*** (These figures do not include those who are employed and run a small business in their spare time).

The following details serve to give you an overview of what you need to consider when deciding upon the right structure for your business.

### Sole Trader

This is the simplest way to set up in business and once you have registered with HMRC you can begin to trade straight away, taking into account any specific licences you might need to consider in your line of work. As a sole trader, you have complete control over your business and accounting affairs. Unlike Limited Companies, you will not need to notify Companies House or deal with any administrative or accounting requirements.

You will, however, be personally liable for any debts you incur in the running of your business and you will also be required to pay Income Tax and National Insurance on these profits. Losses can be offset against tax on any other income, where applicable.

You will be sent a Self-assessment tax form by HMRC in the April after your business starts and you will be liable to pay

Class 2 National Insurance contributions. (£2.40 per week for 2009/2010 tax year).

You will only need to register for VAT when your business turnover (i.e. money coming in from the sale of good and

---

**        reference source The Small Business service—Statistical press release 2001

services your business provides) is in excess of £70,000 per annum. (HM Revenue and Customs).

Other considerations when trading as a sole trader will be covered later such as taking out relevant insurance, opening a business bank account and employing a reputable accountant.

## LIMITED COMPANY

The term 'Limited' refers to the fact that the Company's finances are distinct from the personal finances of their owners, unlike the Sole Trader arrangement.

Tax legislation over the past 10 years has made it less attractive to set up as a Limited Company, unless you are in a type of business that might leave you legally at risk as a debtor.

A Limited Company has a distinct identity from that of the shareholders who are its owners. Therefore, if a Limited Company goes bankrupt, any claims made by its creditors are just limited to the assets of the company.

Limited Companies must:

+ Register with Companies House
+ File annual accounts with Companies House
+ Send an annual return to Companies House (this includes details about key personnel employed, the registered office, share capital and shareholders
+ Inform HMRC of any annual profits or taxable income

- Complete an annual HMRC Corporation Tax Return and pay any tax due within 9 months of the companies year end.

- Ensure any employees pay National Insurance and Income tax on their income.

## PARTNERSHIP

This business structure gives those wanting to set up in business with a partner or two, without any of the legal confines of a Limited Company. Unlike the Limited Company set up, a partnership has no legal standing and is a simpler way of linking two or more people together in a business structure.

Unlike Limited Companies, Partners are personally liable for any debts incurred in the running of the business but a partnership does not need to notify Companies House or deal with any of the administrative or accounting requirements of Limited Companies. Each partner must inform HMRC of their self-employed status and if either partner withdraws from the business, (due to death, resignation or bankruptcy), the partnership must be dissolved immediately as it has no legal status.

If you are feeling somewhat overwhelmed by all the above information and are not sure which business status is right for you, seek professional advice. There are plenty of organisations (such as Business Link) who will give you free and impartial advice.

(STEP 7 identifies useful websites).

## EMPLOYING PEOPLE

As a new business owner, employing people can ease your workload, but you will need to be aware of the regulations and legislation you are required to comply with when employing others.

As it is assumed most readers will be initially considering 'going it alone' in business, such considerations will be covered in more detail in **STEP 6**—Rules and Regulations.

However, at this stage of planning for your business, it is a good idea to be aware of the likelihood of having to employ staff at a later date, once your business has grown, and what the implications are to your particular business.

Just as **YOU** represent your business, it is vital that you choose people whom you can trust and who can be relied upon. Although the 'final buck' ultimately stops with you, it is crucial that your employees represent you and your business in ways that you consider to be essential. There is an old saying that 'you are only as good as your staff' whom you will want to have good, sound qualities such as being responsible, trustworthy and reliable, (to name but a few).

It is also worthwhile remembering that anyone you employ, no matter how good they are at their job, will not necessarily view your business in the same way as you do. There will be times when you will feel that you are living, eating and breathing your business but it is not fair to expect the same of your staff!

On a practical level, if you **are** considering employing staff from the outset, you will need to weigh up what this will cost you and also determine how many hours you will require your staff to work and whether you prefer to have younger staff who you might need to train and keep a watchful eye on but only need to pay the minimum wage or to pay more for more reliable and experienced employees.

You also need to think carefully about the duties they will be expected to perform and an ideal personal profile. Such considerations can be included in your business plan (**see STEP 3**).

As well as employees being a major resource within your business, you will also need to consider all the supplies, materials and equipment you will need. This can include anything from your printed letter-headed paper and relevant stationery to shop fittings, merchandise and equipment. In the case of a café, for example, this would include everything from cutlery, crockery, glassware, furniture, kitchen equipment, soft furnishings, cash registers and so on.

Part of the fun in setting up your own business is to research and source all such materials and you will find a template below for you to keep a record of what you will need to consider buying (or renting/leasing). You can add to this as time goes on; there will always be something you have overlooked and it is one way of attempting to ensure you have thought of everything!

# ACTIVITY 4—
# WHAT I NEED TO BUY

List all the supplies and materials you will need to buy below. This includes not only saleable items but every item you need to set up your business.

It is a good idea to shop around and look at different suppliers to compare prices. Don't be afraid to barter with suppliers; if you don't ask, you don't get!!

Use the following chart to help you identify what items you need to buy. Research several suppliers in order to obtain the best deals.

| item | supplier | expected delivery waiting time | cost |
|---|---|---|---|
|  |  |  |  |
|  |  |  |  |
|  |  |  |  |
|  |  |  |  |
|  |  |  |  |
|  |  |  |  |
|  |  |  |  |
|  |  |  |  |
|  |  |  |  |

Finally it is often a good idea to devise a means of keeping track of all the stages, activities and deadlines from the start of planning your business to your date of opening or when you begin trading.

For some this takes the form of using a diary, for others it consists of using white boards, lists or drawing up a 'timeline'. Whatever method you use is unimportant. What **IS** important however is to ensure you have thought of everything, put all activities into a logical order and set deadline dates beside each one.

## ACTIVITY 5— 
## PLAN OF ACTION

Now devise your own plan of action in whatever format suits you best. Whether you prefer to write your plan on paper, (in the form of a timeline, lists or a diagram), or produce something electronically, the important thing is to have a plan of SOME description--it really does focus the mind on what needs to be achieved!

Do remember that unexpected situations can and will occur for even the most organised of people, so look on the method you use to set out what needs to be done as a 'work in progress' and allow for a certain amount of flexibility to deal with unexpected situations outside your control.

# STEP 2 ACTION POINTS

◊ Activity 1—Initial planning questions to consider

◊ Activity 2—Your market

◊ Activity 3—Where will your business be located?

◊ Activity 4—What do you need to buy?

◊ Activity 5—Plan of action

# STEP 3 ---
## Marketing and why it is essential for the survival of your business

*'You can have brilliant ideas, but if you cannot get
them across, your ideas will not get you anywhere'*

*Lee Iacocca*

It is frequently stated in the business world that if you get
your marketing right, you are well on your way to making your
business venture a successful one.

Marketing is THE ONE most important thing you can
do in your business. It is key to the success of your business
and not just something you 'do' at the setting up stage. As 85%
of start-up businesses don't survive the first three years and
90% of new products fail, it is important not to underestimate
the significance of marketing to your business.

## So what exactly IS marketing?

**Definition:-**

**'Successful marketing is about giving
customers a product or service that meets
their needs at a profit to your business'**

**Mary Munley-The Flying Marketeer.**

People often assume selling and advertising are the same
as marketing but in fact marketing is not a specialist activity at
all, it encompasses the entire business. It is the whole business
seen from the customer's point of view.

Put simply, before you attract customers and therefore
achieve sales, you have to attract people's attention and get
them to contact you in some way and marketing is just that.
It is a continual process and your marketing activities need

to be consistent, appropriate and revised regularly, in order to respond to the requirements of your target audience or 'market'.

A useful way of viewing the significance of marketing to your business is to think of your marketing as a long pipeline into which you are constantly feeding liquid. The pipeline is your business and the liquid represents what you are doing, in a marketing sense, to keep the business going. To begin with, you pump liquid (marketing activities) into your pipeline (your business) at one end and nothing appears at the other end of the pipeline until you continuously pump in the liquid. At first there is a trickle of liquid at the other end, so you need to keep pumping it in, until there is a constant flow coming out at the other end. It is only when the pipeline is continually full that you will get the same output as input!

Your effective early marketing fills the pipeline but remember, if you stop pumping, your pipeline will dry up and you will have to start again. In reality this means your business is not generating the volume of sales that you want and need!

It is recommended that you spend 40% of your time on marketing activities for your business and STEP 3 examines the key activities to be taken into consideration.

# ACTIVITY 1…
## DEVELOP YOUR MARKETING MIND!

As a starting point, (and to show what Marketing means to your business in reality), consider these questions:-

+ What image do you want your business to portray?

+ Will your business name represent this image?

+ Will your name be unique/something no-one else has thought of?

+ Will your logo match the points above?

+ Will all your printed materials look professional and tell the reader what you want them to understand about your business?

+ What advertising do you intend to do?

+ How much will this cost?

+ What promotional activities will you decide on?

## KNOW YOUR MARKET—WHO DO YOU WANT YOUR IDEAL CUSTOMERS TO BE?

Do you know who your customers will be in terms of age, location and income?

It is not enough be passionate about your products and services, you will need to be aware of who you want to attract and, more importantly, who you will **actually** attract. Marketing is often referred to as being all about 'supply and demand'-- giving people what they want--but you will firstly need to discover what and where the demand is. You need give this serious consideration as it will impact on how you develop and implement your marketing activities.

## ACTIVITY 2…
### WHO DO YOU WANT TO ATTRACT TO YOUR BUSINESS AND WHY?

Give this question the time and thought it deserves; it is simply not enough to feel you have a great idea and that everyone will want to but what you have to offer

Will what your business conveys stand up amongst your competitors and attract the kind of customers you want?

Will what you have to offer send out the correct messages to your prospective customers in order that they buy from **you** and not someone else?

By knowing who your target audience is you can then develop your business image and brand to meet their needs. If this is not consistent and appropriate, it will send out the wrong messages.

(This will be more fully explained in the Marketing Mix section).

So be very aware of WHO your business will be targeting and your reasons for this.

## UNDERTAKE SOME APPROPRIATE MARKET RESEARCH

Not only do you need to understand WHO your customer is, you also need to know WHAT they want, before setting up your business. It is therefore very important to spend time researching your market (your 'market' being the people you want to attract to buy from you and your business).

Without going into technical details of the different types of marketing research, here is a list of the main ways of undertaking market research:-

+ Face to face interviews
+ Mystery shoppers
+ Focus groups
+ Surveys
+ Trade associations
+ Trade magazines
+ Trade fairs and events
+ Websites
+ Informal contacts/networking
+ Using government data
+ Using electoral roles
+ Looking at information held by trade and professional bodies

- ✦ Looking at consumer surveys and reports (e.g. Mintel)

There are many different market research activities and larger companies and organisations often invest in market research specialists to undertake marketing research on their behalf. However, for those setting up a small business, this need not be as daunting an activity as it sounds. In fact, it can be great fun!

Remember the marketing pipeline? Never bypass a marketing opportunity-- research other people in the same line of work as you, ask your friends and family about what they are looking for from a business like yours and visit competitor's websites to see what they have to offer—their prices, their products & the language they use to attract their target audience.

Market research is important; it enables you to discover who your main competitor's are-- what they have to offer, where they are located, what they specialise in and what you can do differently or better.

## ACTIVITY 3...

### LIST THE TYPES OF MARKETING RESEARCH YOU ARE GOING TO UNDERTAKE AND WRITE DOWN WHAT YOUR INVESTIGATIONS REVEAL

For example, if you wanted to open a tea shop in your nearest local town, you could scour all the local magazines, newspapers and look at competitors websites to get a 'feel' of what they offer, and the prices they charge.

You could also act as a 'mystery shopper' in your local and surrounding town's cafes and note what the décor is like, what is on the menu, the prices, how welcoming the staff are, where it is located  and what, if anything, made this café stick out from it's competitors. This will help you consider your USP (see below) and guide you to make some informed decisions about how you will develop and introduce your business in order to create the sales you expect and hope for.

Consider:-

+ Which type of research will you decide to use?

+ Where will you get any required information from?

+ Who can you talk to whose information will be useful and relevant?

+ What organisations and associations could you join?

All such research is valuable; not only will it give you a true picture of what you are up against but it will also help you decide on what you need to offer that is perhaps different in an increasingly competitive market and, when it comes to writing a business plan, you will have already done much of the ground work needed for the marketing section!!

## Your USP—Unique Selling Proposition/Point

Unless you have hit upon a completely new service/product/idea for your business, the chances are that there will be others offering something very similar to yourself. Competition can be a positive rather than negative aspect of business, as long as you are offering what your customers want. But what if you can offer them something slightly different? Will you have a UNIQUE SELLING PROPOSITION/POINT? (**USP**)

### By identifying what it is your customers want, you will be able to develop your own unique offering.

A USP can be something as simple as offering your customers a completely different product or service from your competitors at a similar price to the existing market.

You may not remember a time when garages just sold petrol or supermarkets only sold food? Now all the well known garages and supermarkets are offering a whole lot more! But one had to make the first move and so create a captive audience.

And what about the days before mobile phones, Nintendo's, W.I.'s and microwaves were introduced? Your USP does not have to be a new invention, just something you can provide that no one else is offering.

If you are not sure what your USP might be at this stage,

here are some tips for developing your USP from the online networking organisation **Enterprising Women**.

+ Look at and analyse your competitors. Choose six and identify their USP. What are their strengths and weaknesses?

+ Brainstorm your USP ideas with others. Don't judge their views and write them down. Get feedback from as many other people as you can.

+ Narrow your USP concept down to a single, main, concept that is different from others. (This need not be complicated, it might be that you offer a monthly 'themed' evening in your café, for example, as no one else does this locally).

+ Make sure your USP is relevant to your customers and fulfils their needs. Ask yourself-- will your future customers/clients pay for it?!

+ Develop a 'tagline/strapline/slogan/mission statement and be prepared to use it on all advertising and marketing e.g. your website, letterheads, compliment slips, business cards, flyers etc

## ACTIVITY 4…
### DESCRIBE WHAT YOUR USP MIGHT BE AND DEVELOP A SLOGAN/MISSION STATEMENT

Having researched your competitors, you will now have more of an idea of what others are saying and using to promote their business. What do you want to be remembered for and can you fully identify with it?

My USP is

-------------------------------------------------------------------------------

# 4 MARKETING SWOT ANALYSIS

SWOT stands for:-

**S**trengths, **W**eaknesses, **O**pportunities **and** Threats

The strengths and weaknesses refer to you or the 'internal parts' of the business and the opportunities and threat refer to the external aspects of the business.

A SWOT analysis not only helps you to focus on what forms of marketing activity will be appropriate for your business but it also raises awareness of what YOU might need to work on internally and external.

There is an example of a swot analysis on the following page.

| INTERNAL FACTORS | |
| --- | --- |
| **STRENGTHS** | **WEAKNESSES** |
| You will promise & over deliver with excellent customer service<br><br>You will have a prime location site<br><br>You will offer high quality products<br><br>You will strive to build an excellent reputation in your field | You have lack of marketing expertise<br><br>You lack of management expertise<br><br>You have insufficient funds to self-finance |
| **OPPORTUNITIES** | **THREATS** |
| You could develop other products in association with your key business areas<br><br>You could move into a new market segment as your business grows<br><br>You could expand into national and maybe international sales in the future by introducing online sales | Price wars from competitors<br><br>A new competitor moves into your area<br><br>An existing competitor introduces a successful new product |
| EXTERNAL FACTORS | |

The benefits of completing a SWOT analysis is that it raises awareness, both regarding your own capabilities and it also allows you to consider what is out there with regard to your competitors and the business environment. You will be able to build on your strengths and, in the case of the weaknesses given in the example above, it may just be a case of seeking professional advice (which can often be free!) and producing a sound business plan, (see **STEP** 5), in order to raise the necessary finance to fund your business.

## SWOT TIPS

- Be realistic with your strengths and weaknesses
- SWOT should distinguish between where your business is today and where it could be in the future
- SWOT should be specific
- SWOT should be kept simple
- SWOT is subjective
- Always apply SWOT in relation to your competitors.

# ACTIVITY 5...
## COMPLETE YOUR OWN SWOT ANALYSIS

| STRENGTHS | WEAKNESSES |
|---|---|
|  |  |
| **OPPORTUNITIES** | **THREATS** |
|  |  |

## THE MARKETING MIX

The chartered Institute of marketing defines Marketing as having:-

## 'THE RIGHT PRODUCT, IN THE RIGHT PLACE, AT THE RIGHT TIME AND AT THE RIGHT PLACE'.

Once you have identified your target audience/market and discovered who your competitors are, you need to think about your marketing mix.

This is where you ensure all aspects of your business are consistent and sends out the desired messages to attract your targeted customers.

You can look on the 4 P's of the marketing mix-- **Product, Price**, **Place & Promotion** --as being a bit like an artist's palette. You can mix up the four 'colours' in different quantities to deliver a final colour. Every painting is original in some way and the same can be said about the marketing mix.

The marketing mix is not as complex as it sounds and many people who have carefully considered all aspects of their business will strive to make sure it all 'matches' properly like pieces in a jigsaw puzzle.

The 4 'P's' should not be seen as static and its elements may need to be altered in order to keep up with customer demands and trends, the competition and economic considerations.

As an example of the latter, when a new Disability Law was introduced in the late 1990's, it meant many businesses were required to change their premises (e.g. introduce disabled toilets) and revise their employee structure to comply with the law which in turn meant spending money they did not necessarily have to spend or which had been earmarked for something else in their business.

This is an ideal example of a 'threat' to business in the previous SWOT exercise

MacDonald's have always kept abreast with their marketing strategy, changing their marketing mix to keep abreast of their customers, competitors and economic trends. They always offer a no-frills, fast-food alternative to other take-away outlets, positioning themselves in well-located areas and keeping their prices very competitive. They were the first of their kind to give away toys to children, have drive-through facilities and keep up with national trends such as healthy eating and recycling. They always appear to be one step ahead of their competitors & this will undoubtedly be down to stringent marketing research and continually revising their marketing mix.

When you decide on YOUR mix, be ever mindful of what message you are giving out to your current & prospective customers.

Would you expect to buy an expensive perfume in a cheap brown cardboard box for example?

Would you expect to find a mass produced, cheap plastic purse in a designer shop selling at the same price as a leather one?

As stated earlier, it's all about keeping everything you convey to your customers about your business consistent, appropriate and relevant.

## PRICE

There are many ways to price a product/service & it is advisable to research your competitors pricing structure as well as seeking advice from established business owners & experts but here are 2 main ways to price a product/service:-

1.  Setting a higher price than your main competitors when offering a unique product/service (e.g. bespoke leather shoes, cruises)

2.  Using a lower price than your competitors in order to gain a share of their market (e.g. Sky TV offering a low introductory price).

Don't forget to keep abreast of market trends and offer promotional prices when appropriate.

You will also want to maintain customer loyalty as well as attracting new customers, so what incentive schemes might you introduce to keep your customers coming back to you? (e.g. if you get referred trade from a customer, what 'reward' can you give them for giving you new business?).

## PLACE

This is not just referring to where you locate your business, (although get this wrong & it can have a serious knock-on effect to the flow of customer traffic to your establishment), but it also relates to how you sell your products and services (e.g. retail, wholesale, online, locally, nationally or internationally) and also where you get your supplies from—wholesalers, agents, retailers etc. The cost of your key business supplies will affect the price you can sell your goods to your customers.

It is therefore important not only to think long and hard as to how you are going to 'position' your business but also to research your suppliers very carefully and to monitor these costs on a regular basis, so that you can make informed decisions as to when to change/ challenge existing suppliers.

## PRODUCT

It is always important to be aware of a product's popularity and to make changes to what you sell/offer as market forces dictate.

Looking back at what McDonald's have introduced and rejected in their product range over the years has seen pizzas come and go in a very short space of time, salads to be introduced, phased out and then re-introduced again and portions of fresh fruit suddenly introduced at the time when we were first being encouraged to eat five portions of fruit and vegetables a day.

The product part of the marketing mix also looks at what materials, designs and technology is used to make your products more attractive and believable for your customers. If, for instance, you want your business to have an environmental awareness, a business card using re-cycled paper and stating as such, would give you more credibility. Or if you aim to give a percentage of your profits to a local charity, make sure you have links to the charities' website and visa versa as well as promoting any related activities you have been involved in.

## PROMOTION

Finally we come to the aspect of marketing which many people often confuse with being the sum total of what marketing is all about; how you make people aware of what it is you are offering in order that they buy from you and not someone else.

It is essential you are very clear from the outset what you are selling in order to know where to go in order to promote your goods and services in an appropriate way. Would it be wise, for example, to advertise luxury spa breaks for adults in a children's magazine? Or to offer reduced price Master's degree courses in The Sun or Daily Mirror?

Key promotional activities are:-

+ Personal selling
+ Special offers/promotions
+ Advertising
+ Public relations and publicity stunts
+ Direct mail (eg- inserts in magazines/newspapers, flyers, coupons, leaflet drops, internet, mail shots).
+ An easy to navigate website
+ Networking

Everything and anything seen by your customers must be consistent otherwise you will send out mixed and confusing messages about what your business is all about and, more importantly, why those customers should buy from you and not one of your competitors.

This is not just ensuring that your printed materials match and convey what you want to say about your business in order to attract your ideal customers but it is also about you as an individual. If your website states that you offer a professional service, this also takes into consideration the impression you give: do you always turn up for appointments on time? Do you reply to emails straight away? Do you deliver what you promise and even go the extra mile? Do you dress appropriately?

One of the things new business owners frequently lament is that they have spent a great deal of their marketing budget on advertising and seen little or no return for their investment.

It is therefore worth taking note of Chris Cardell's advice: (www.marketingessentials.co.uk):-

**'You should never spend more than you can afford to lose on a new advertising campaign.'**

Just remember to think about what your marketing mix says about you and your business and will you attract those customers you are aiming for.

At this point it is worth mentioning that some marketing experts also include a fifth 'P' to the mix: **PEOPLE.** Your business will only be as good as the staff you employ, (particularly if you are offering a service), so it essential you choose reliable employees who will totally represent what your business stands for.

You will also reap the benefits of meeting lots of different people who may either use your products and services themselves, or, given time in getting to know you and what your business is all about, may recommend you to others. The value of social networking to your business, both in person and online (with the likes of Twitter, Facebook and LinkedIn), cannot be underestimated. Social networking is now such a viable marketing tool as people always ultimately buy from other people and it is your chance to give the right impression and convince others you can offer them what they want. A word of warning though, networking is part of the marketing pipeline and as such should be included as a regular marketing activity in order to build up awareness about your business.

Many new small business owners shy away from networking events because they dread having to stand up and give a minutes' presentation about their business. However it is worth remembering that everyone has to do the same thing and, as with anything in life, practice makes perfect!

There is a concept that you are only 6 people away from the person you need to make contact with, (the 6 degrees of separation, also referred to as The Human Web and devised by Frigyes Karinthy). One of the great things about networking is that you never know who you will meet that may help your business or someone else's and this aspect far outweighs any discomfort you may feel when standing up for a minute and selling your business to a captive audience!

<u>ACTIVITY 6...</u>
# <u>YOUR MARKETING MIX</u>

Using a form similar to the one below, (or a list will do equally as well), begin to think about what YOUR business' marketing mix will be. Again, this is a useful exercise as it will be included in your business plan.

| | |
|---|---|
| **Price** | |
| **Place** | |
| **Product** | |
| **Promotion** | |

## <u>MARKETING OBJECTIVES/GOALS</u>

It is important to devise a set of short, medium & long term marketing goals as your business develops. This allows you to be able to 'step outside the box' and consider what you need to spend in order to take your business further and how you are going to raise awareness in order to justify such expenditure.

As a guideline, make sure your marketing objectives are **SMART:-**

**S**PECIFIC be precise about what you are going to achieve

**ME**ASURABLE quantify your objectives/goals

**A**CHIEVABLE are you attempting too much?

**R**EALISTIC do you have the resources to make your objectives happen?

**T**IMED state WHEN you will achieve your objectives

It is always a good idea to have a timeline or plan of action of all the activities you need to undertake in order to open on time and by setting goals and giving them dates for completion (which CAN be changed according to circumstances), you are more likely to achieve what you set out to achieve rather than leaving things to chance. This may seem obvious but it is surprising how few people actually set goals with deadlines.

## Activity 7…
# SETTING GOALS WITH TIMELINES

A good starting point is to start from the end ie when you want to launch your business. How you decide to organise this is up to you but it may help to make a list of everything you need to do to prepare for your business start date and then plan week by week, month by month, in practical terms, of what you need to do in order to make it all happen.

You will find this is work in progress and will be constantly changing, this is where you need focus, determination and resilience.

As an example, here is a list of everything you might need to consider when opening the previously mentioned café. Let's assume the owner has done their research, decided on their marketing mix and the aim is for the café to operate from a small, rented shop in a local town with the owner wishing to employ 2 part-time staff to begin with.

+ Decide on a business name and strap line
+ Research suitable properties via estate agents, the internet and local papers
+ View properties, find out about cost and time scales for connecting utilities
+ Decide on branding (logo, printed materials etc)—research and meet printers, designers
+ Get all promotional materials printed
+ Create website-undergo training or research and meet suitable web designers, buy web domain name

- Research and contact appropriate bodies regarding Health & Safety, legal requirements, planning applications etc

- Plan menus, prices, opening times

- Research, contact and compare suppliers (refer to activity 4, STEP 2)

- Place orders to be ready for launch date

- Write business plan

- Research sources of finance

- Arrange an appointment with the bank manager

- Decide on type and cost of advertising and promotion—low key or an official opening by invitation? Press releases? Leaflet drops? Local newspaper promotion

- Advertise for staff

- Recruit and train staff

- Other

This list is meant to act purely as an example and is not in any particular order. You will need to think of other considerations as appropriate to your business and also put into priority as far as short, medium and long term aims are concerned.

Whilst you may feel overwhelmed by all the marketing considerations to be taken into account, it is important to put things into perspective. You will not have entered into setting up your own business in a light-hearted way and therefore it is important to take time to do your planning, research and organisation at a pace that is best suited to you.

# STEP 3 ACTION POINTS

◊  **Activity 1**—Develop your marketing mind

◊  **Activity 2**—Who you want to attract to your
business and why

◊  **Activity 3**—Your marketing research
activities

◊  **Activity 4**—Your USP and slogan

◊  **Activity 5**—Your SWOT analysis

◊  **Activity 6**—Your marketing mix

◊  **Activity 7**—Your goals and timescales

# STEP 4
# Cash Is King—an overview of all things financial

*Becoming wealthy is not a matter of how much you
earn, who your parents are or what you do. It is
a matter of managing your money properly.*

*Noel Whittaker.*

It is a common misconception that a great deal of money is required to set up a small business. Obviously it is an entirely different matter if you are thinking of opening a large factory, employing several people or if you plan to purchase several pieces of machinery and equipment. But generally speaking, there is a lot to be said for starting up your business within your financial means.

With an increasing number of people working from home, job sharing and flexi-time, it is possible to set up a small business whilst still working in paid employment and taking care to set realistic short, medium and log-term goals, thus allowing you to expand your business once your financial returns give you the wherewithal to do so.

It is equally possible to set up your business for a relatively small initial outlay.

Just as your business acumen and expertise grow, hopefully your bank balance will as well. Make use of your network of useful professional contacts (friends, family and recommendations) and you may consider 'trading-in' of skills and services in the early stages. Perhaps your newly appointed sole trader accountant, (who came highly recommended to you), may see fit to give you a healthy reduction in their fees in return for benefiting from the goods or services your business provides. Or perhaps you have met a marketing expert who would willingly trade his or her skills in return for your IT expertise.

It requires a certain amount of tenacity and thinking 'outside the box,' but it can be surprising how asking for what you require and keeping in regular touch with mutually useful and like-minded people, can help when you are first setting up in business.

## FUNDING

It may seem obvious that the more planning you do initially to assess your financial requirements, the more likely it will be that you don't experience financial difficulties later, but it is surprising how many people do not fully consider their finances prior to trading.

Before you decide how you will raise the money required, (assuming you do not have sufficient, independently acquired funds yourself), be sure to ask yourself some key questions:-

- What are your initial and ongoing costs going to be—resources, employees, equipment, premises, utilities, rent and rates, marketing, promotion, advertising, insurances, private pension, website design etc?

- How much money will you need to make each week and month to cover your personal and business expenses?

- What will you charge for your products or services?

- What form of book-keeping system will you use to keep track of your income and outgoings on a daily basis?

+ How will you support yourself while starting up the business?

(Known as 'working capital', many people do not allow for funds to tide them over while their business is in its early stages of growth. It may well take a year of trading or more before the business experiences the desired turnover).

+ Will you need to allow for any training costs?

+ Will you need to allow for any further development costs?

+ Will you have a contingency fund to allow for unexpected expenses?

Even if you are in a fortunate position to self-finance your start-up business, it is still wise to compile a business plan. (Step 5 covers the key considerations when compiling a business plan). This will certainly be a requirement for anyone seeking external funding, (a bank loan, an overdraft or credit), but it will also prove to be a very worthwhile activity to keep you focused on all aspects of what your business is about, taking into account all the key considerations, and allowing you to make realistic financial forecasting and planning.

You will discover most of the information required for compiling a business plan, will have already been covered in STEP 3!

## What kind of funding is available?

### Bank Loans

It is wise to shop around the various high street banks to compare what products and services they offer. Most will provide free start up guides and business planning advice and some provide free seminars and workshops for new businesses. Find out what free banking they offer (usually between one to two years, depending on the bank), and find out if you will have an individual assigned to you to answer any queries as they arise. Some banks supply a relationship manager who offers free business advice.

It is also crucial that you fully understand the terms of any loan or overdraft offered. Many banks will expect security for any money they lend you such as a personal guarantee or business assets and you may well have to invest some of your own money into the business in order to secure a loan. Always seek advice from your accountant or business advisor in order to ensure that any borrowing meets your requirements and that you understand the terms, before signing any agreement.

Whatever type of borrowing you use, you may have to pay arrangement fees as well as interest. Some small businesses find an overdraft facility sufficient to cover their borrowing needs whilst a loan may be more feasible for longer term financing.

### Credit cards

Many small start up businesses use a credit card to initially fund expenses such as travel, stationery and fuel. However, it is unwise to rely totally on credit cards as a means of borrowing money, as interest charges can be relatively high.

## BUSINESS ANGELS

Business angels are individuals or syndicates who invest in high growth businesses in return for equity; usually 20-49% of the business, depending on the investment. Those of you who have watched the popular TV series-'Dragons Den'- will be aware that you must have a sound business idea as well as being able to 'pitch' your business in a convincing, professional and realistic way!

Business angels will often make their contacts, skills and experience available to the company they invest in.

## GOVERNMENT GRANTS

There is a range of government support available to people wanting to set up their own business. The local council will have a list of what is available. Grants of between £500 -£1000 are typical amounts, but some businesses may be able to apply for multiple grants. Government grants are almost always awarded for a specific proposed business and not for existing businesses.

Factors which determine eligibility for grants are:-

+ **Size**—usually issued to start up businesses
+ **Location**-a business located in an area undergoing regeneration is more likely to receive funding
+ **Sector-** grants available will depend not only on the location but also what industry you represent

You will be expected to produce a business plan outlining how much money you will need and whether there is a market for your type of business. (Contact your local Business Link office who should be able to assist with potential sources of help from central and local government as well as private organisations. (**See STEP 7 useful websites**)

## The Enterprise Finance Guarantee Scheme

Under this scheme, the UK Department for Business Innovation & Skills (BIS), guarantees 75% of your loan which means you do not need a large amount of security to back your borrowing.

## Types of business costs

There are four main types of business costs:-

1.  **Variable costs** —these relate to the sales you make such as the raw materials you need for the production process and the goods you buy in and then resell.

2.  **Fixed costs** – these do not vary directly in relation to your sales and will usually be monthly or annual expenses such as wages, insurance, rent and utility bills.

3.  **Capital costs** – these relate to the purchase of business assets such as computers and vehicles and occur relatively infrequently.

4.  **Government taxes** – these relate to costs such as VAT (if you are VAT registered), employee PAYE and National Insurance contributions.

# ACTIVITY 1—
# HOW MUCH TO BORROW AND WHO TO BORROW FROM?

It is essential you calculate accurately how much money you need to borrow and where that money will come from. Do not under estimate your borrowing requirement. There will always be hidden expenses you have not accounted for, not forgetting to allow for funds to tide you over at the start before you begin to generate sales!

It may not be necessary to buy all your equipment new; why not, for example, look into second-hand and leasing opportunities?

### A- Draw up a List of setting up and ongoing costs.

*(refer to your list in activity 4, STEP 2 for general supplies and materials. This is an example and by no means a definitive list, as each business will have specific requirements).*

|  | Initial Costs | Ongoing Costs |
|---|---|---|
| property/rent |  |  |
| rates |  |  |
| equipment/plant/machinery |  |  |
| motor expenses |  |  |
| printing, packaging, stationery |  |  |
| advertising, marketing |  |  |
| website design |  |  |
| professional fees (e.g. accountant) |  |  |
| employees |  |  |
| insurance(s) |  |  |
| bank charges, loans, interest |  |  |
| initial stock |  |  |
| miscellaneous (itemise) |  |  |

## B~ RESEARCH SOURCES OF FINANCE AND LIST RESULTS

By listing what each lender offers, you will be able to compare which most appropriately suit your business and personal needs.

**Example:-**

| Lender | £ borrowed | loan terms | pros | cons |
|---|---|---|---|---|
| Nat West | £20,000 |  |  |  |

## CASH FLOW FORECASTING

Planning your cash requirements for your business is a vital consideration for every self-employed person. Whilst it is possible to be trading profitably, if there is not enough cash available to pay for ongoing expenses such as the tax bill, rent or wages because financial resources are tied up in equipment and stock on the shelves, the results can be disastrous.

When people talk about having cash flow problems, it is often a case of having made a decision to buy a quantity of stock or supplies at a bargain price only to find sales do not happen at the anticipated rate. Unless you offer a service rather than supplying goods, it is likely you will have to buy stock/goods long before customers buy from you and stock on the shelves could otherwise be money in the bank. Knowing what your cash requirements are will allow you to make informed decisions as to what sort of work/contracts you can take on.

Be mindful of the fact that your suppliers are likely to demand their payments before you are in a position to forward your bills to your customers. Good cash flow is defined by a pattern of income and spending that allows a business to have cash available to pay bills and wages on time.

In order to forecast your cash flow budget you need to take into consideration what money you are likely to have coming into and out of your business over a period of time.

## 7 KEY STEPS TO TAKE WHEN CASH FLOW FORECASTING*.

(*Source:- www.businesslink.gov.uk).

**Step 1** - produce a cash flow forecast for the next 12 months. Estimate the split of credit and cash sales and the credit period taken by your customers so that receipts are put in the correct month.

**Step 2** – Establish whether any other cash income will be received. This will include money you are investing in your business as well as loans and grants where applicable.

**Step 3** – Decide what purchases you will need to make to achieve your sales forecast. Your suppliers may want payment in cash initially, but after a month or two, may set up a trade account and you will then benefit from credit terms.

**Step 4** – Identify your other regular monthly cash payments.

**Step 5** – Identify any one-off expenditure such as fixed asset purchases.

**Step 6** – Set out the cash flow forecast month by month for a full year. Always make sure your figures correspond to when you expect payments to be actually made.

**Step 7** – List your assumptions as a reminder of how you have derived your figures—for example, payment terms and cash cycle length used. Most lenders will want to review your assumptions as these will help them to identify whether your figures have been thought through in detail.

Once you have completed your cash flow forecast, you need to compare it with what happens in reality.

**An example of a simple cash-flow forecast**.

| (A) RECEIPTS | pre-start-up | months: 1 to 12 |
|---|---|---|
| Cash in hand | | |
| Cash sales | | |
| Capital | | |
| | | |
| | | |
| Total receipts (A) | | |

## (B)PAYMENTS

Payments

Stock

Wages

Rent

Rates

Water

Telephone

Electricity/gas

Maintenance and repairs

Postage./printing/stationery

Marketing/advertising

Website charges

Professional fees

Loan repayments

Bank interest charges

Car/petrol expenses

VAT

Total payments (B)

Net cash flow (A-B)

Opening balance

Closing balance

## Book keeping and accounting systems

Many accountants recount stories of their customers presenting them with their years 'accounts' in the form of a scruffy plastic bag containing a pile of receipts and invoices in no particular order! Many banks will also relate that at least 80% of all business failures are caused by inadequate record keeping. Even if you choose to invest in the services of an accountant, they will still expect, (not unreasonably), a basic form of record keeping which shows all monies paid into and out of the business. There are numerous templates available online and your accountant will advise you as to the most acceptable format to use.

As stated before, it is advisable to seek professional advice, but if your business is very small and operates a very simple form of trading, the following will explain what you need to consider for our bookkeeping/accountancy records.

## Keep all purchase receipts

Get into the habit of keeping and filing all receipts for anything you buy for your business. You can always throw away anything that cannot be claimed as a business expense. You will need to complete a tax return each financial year and whether you do this yourself or employ the services of an accountant to do it for you, by adopting a workable system at the beginning, it will be less of a time consuming task when you have to tally everything up at the end of your financial year. An expandable wallet with 12 sections can be used to put all your receipts in or use a folder, using plastic wallets for each month of the year.

## CASH BOOK

A simple notebook is all you need in order to keep a record of all sales and expenditure. Not only will your accountant or book keeper need this record to compile your accounts, but it is a means of keeping a monthly track of what your sales and expenses are, especially if the two columns are side by side and you notice that you are spending more than you are taking in any one month!

To make sure everything matches the invoices you send out or purchases you make, it is a good idea to include invoice numbers, cheque numbers and dates of receipts within your cash book.

Generally speaking, if you take time to devise a system that you can work with from the beginning, it will save you time in the long run.

If you decide to use a spreadsheet to record all transactions do be aware that computers can and do crash, so make sure you keep back up records at all times.

## VAT RECORDS

You will be required to register for VAT if you supply goods or services with a value over a certain threshold, (£70,000 in 2010) and you will pay VAT throughout the year at regular intervals. Seek professional advice as to whether or not you should register for VAT as some businesses may gain a tax advantage by registering voluntarily, even if their turnover is below the threshold.

## PROFIT AND LOSS ACCOUNT

Your accountant will draw up a set of accounts from your book keeping records, the first of which is a profit and loss account which illustrates whether you have been making a profit or loss over the year. This is usually produced annually but if you are registered for VAT, quarterly Profit & Loss accounts will enable you to measure your progress when you make your VAT return.

### Example of a simple profit and loss account

|  | £ | £ |
|---|---|---|
| **Sales** |  | 40,000 |
| Purchases | 20,000 |  |
| Opening stock | 2,000 |  |
|  | --------- |  |
|  | 22,000 |  |
| Less Closing Stock | 1,000 | 21,000 |
| **Gross Profit** |  | **19,000** |
| Expenses |  |  |
| Rent and Rates | 2,000 |  |
| Heat and Lighting | 450 |  |
| Telephone | 200 |  |
| Advertising and Marketing | 550 |  |
| Insurance | 150 |  |
| Accountant | 150 |  |
| Travel | 250 | 3,7510 |
| **Net Profit** |  | **15,250** |

## BALANCE SHEET

The balance sheet gives a picture of where the business stands regarding what it owes and what it owns, (assets and liabilities) at a particular point in the year, usually at the end of the company's financial year.

Assets are things or sums of money the business owns.

Fixed assets are items which the business needs in order to operate such as machinery, vehicles, fixtures and fittings. Current assets are things from which cash will be generated in the course of the business' trading activities. As the value of any vehicles will reduce with time, an amount is allowed for 'depreciation' on the balance sheet.

Liabilities are things or amounts the business owes others.

Current liabilities are what the business owes in terms of creditors, credit card balances, loans and HP agreements.

### Example of a simple balance sheet

|  | £ | £ |
|---|---|---|
| **Fixed Assets** |  |  |
| Work Van | 5,000 |  |
| Depreciation | 800 | 4,200 |
| **Current Assets** |  |  |
| Stock | 1,500 |  |
| Trade Debtors | 2,000 | 3,500 |
| **Total Assets** |  | **7,700** |

| | £ | £ |
|---|---|---|
| **Current Liabilities** | | |
| Trade Creditors | 1,700 | |
| Machine HP | 650 | |
| **Total Current Liabilities** | | **2,350** |
| **Capital Account*** | | **5.350** |

(*if the liabilities came to more than the assets, the final figure would be enclosed in brackets to show a minus figure).

## INVOICING

Be sure to create a system that ensures invoices are correct, sent to the right person (not as crazy as it sounds; if you are sending out lots of envelopes in one go, it only takes a moments distraction to put the wrong invoice in an envelope!).

Make sure you have a system in place that can track payments easily as you are likely to be offering a fixed trading period, (for example bills to be paid within 2 working weeks of the date of the invoice) and it is easy to miss items owed without a user -friendly system in place.

## SURVIVAL INCOME

Finally, depending on your personal circumstances, it is important to estimate how much you will need to take as income or 'drawings' from your business. Some new business owners who are supported financially by a partner can afford not to pay themselves a wage until such time as sales increase to an acceptable level. However, for those who are self-supporting, it is vital to estimate what is required in order to survive during the first few months while the business grows.

From Dream To Reality

## Activity 2—
# HOW MUCH DO I NEED TO SURVIVE ON?

This activity will help you work out what your own 'survival level' is; that is, the very least income you will need to have coming in.

| Estimated Expenditure | Monthly | Annual |
|---|---|---|
| Mortgage/rent | | |
| Council tax | | |
| Electricity | | |
| Gas/water/oil | | |
| Telephone | | |
| Insurances | | |
| Car-petrol/services | | |
| HP repayments/loans | | |
| Food | | |
| Household expenses | | |
| Clothing | | |
| Entertainment | | |
| subscriptions | | |
| presents | | |
| other | | |
| **Total expenditure (a)** | | |
| Other income (b) | | |
| **Personal survival income = a-b** | | |

People become self-employed for a variety of reasons but if the key reason is NOT to earn money, it is unlikely your business idea will succeed.

Perhaps you want to reduce your working hours and are happy to take a cut in salary as this will give you the work/life balance you desire. Maybe money is not an issue for you and you want to concentrate on developing a product or service you have felt passionate about for some time. Whatever your reasons are for setting up a business, it is vital to maintain a realistic attitude to money.

# STEP 4 ACTION POINTS

◊ Activity1—how much do you need to borrow?

◊ Activity2—how much do I need to survive on?

# STEP 5

## Producing a Business Plan-----
## it need not be as daunting as
## you think.

**A business plan is primarily an organizing tool used to simplify and clarify business goals and strategies. However, a Business Plan is also a sales tool. If it cannot convince at least one other person of the value of your business idea, then either your business is not worth pursuing or your plan needs major rewriting.**

**PJ Patsula**

If you are looking to borrow money to finance setting up your business, the bank/Building Society you approach for funding will expect comprehensive and detailed information about your proposed business.

Even if you are in the fortunate position of not having to borrow money to set up your business, it is still recommended that you put together a Business Plan as it will set out the vision you have for your business. It will also allow you to outline the purpose of your business and let you set realistic goals. It then becomes a helpful framework for developing your business and for monitoring its progress.

Many professionals will argue that a Business Plan that is well thought out and put together will allow the new business owner to achieve more in terms of time, effort and money in the long term. Look on your Business Plan as a series of goals or stages that you will need to achieve in order to successfully run your own business.

**STEP 2** looked at areas to consider when planning to set up your business. Devising a Business Plan is simply a more detailed examination of those areas. Each stage can be a plan in itself and helps you to focus, in a realistic way, on what needs to be considered, organised and put into place to ensure your business concept is sound, viable and, ultimately, profitable! Even if you don't refer to your Business Plan once your business is up and running, it is surprising how many worthwhile thoughts and ideas can evolve from writing them down in a structured and logical way.

**STEP 5** intends to point you in the right direction with suggestions as to the desirable content your Business Plan should contain.

There is no right way to set out your Business Plan and it is suggested you look at some examples to give you an idea of what to include. All the High Street Banks provide templates for Business Planning and there are websites where sample plans can be downloaded and an appointment with a Business Link Advisor will allow you to get invaluable advice & support.

## Business Plan Content

As stated above, there is no right or wrong way of compiling a Business Plan. These suggested headings serve to give you an idea of what to include and each will be looked at individually.

- Your profile
- Description of your business & its purpose
- Your business vision & long-term objectives
- Current market situation
- Your target customers
- Marketing (covered in section 4)
- SWOT analysis
- Your competitors

+ Financial information

+ SWOT analysis

+ Timeline (optional)

+ Appendices with examples referred to in the in main body of the Business Plan

It is up to you how you approach compiling the content of your Business Plan; some people like to work their way through one section at a time, others like to have several sections on the go at once. It depends on how it works best for you!

Expect to add to, alter, refine and proof read your Business Plan several times before it is in its most presentable state.

## PROFILE

This section allows you to briefly describe you and why you are the right person to set up your proposed business.

As well as giving relevant information, you might want to include an up to date CV (in the appendix), to further qualify what you have written about your skills, capabilities and experience.

**STEP 2** on PLANNING will have already prepared you for providing the necessary information for some of the following activities so make sure you present your details in a way that they describe you in the best possible way.

# ACTIVITY 1

Write an introductory paragraph describing your reasons for wanting to run your proposed business and include your skills, and experience. Aim to be concise, plausible and only include what is relevant. If your business is offering a service, make sure you give some examples of how you are well equipped for running this type of business. What personal qualities can you bring to the role?

## BUSINESS DESCRIPTION AND PURPOSE

This section spells out what your business is and does. The questions below will help you decide what you can include in this section.

- What is the nature of your business?
- What is your business name?
- What legal structure is it? (sole ownership, partnership, limited company) (covered in **STEP 2**)
- Where is the business located and registered?
- When will the business open for business?
- What is the scope of your business? (Local, regional, national, international)
- What are the products and services you will be offering?
- How will you sell and deliver your products to your customers?
- What suppliers will you be using?
- What is your competitive advantage? (Price, location, quality, USP)

◆    What is your business vision?

On the last point, it is vital that your business demonstrates congruence; are all aspects of your business-- the name, the products, the design of your shop, your marketing materials and your prices—all giving the same message?

You will want your business to stand out and have an impact on your customers. Many businesses have a Mission statement. This is a brief sentence or 'strap line' which describes what your business is or does.

Here are some well known examples:

You know you're worth it-- L'Oreal

Every little helps----------- Tesco

I'm loving it--------------- McDonald's

**Example Mission statements:-**

*'McDonald's vision is to be the world's best quick service restaurant experience. Being the best means providing outstanding quality, service, cleanliness and value, so that we make every customer in every restaurant smile.'*

`Do you agree with this statement? Do they deliver what they promise? When the first McDonalds opened in Moscow in the 1980's, it made headline news; the concept of 'fast service' was so new to the Russian public that the queues extended for a considerable distance and it took a long time to serve each customer.

*'Safety, security and consistent delivery of the basics are the foundation of everything we do.'   Virgin Atlantic*

Do Virgin Atlantic deliver what they promise?

# ACTIVITY 2 ~~~
# MY MISSION STATEMENT

Have a go at writing your own mission statement which sums up what your business is offering to your targeted customers.

This is not an easy task and I can guarantee it will take much thought to come up with a sentence which conveys what you and your business is all about. So give it the time it deserves and do not fret if it doesn't come to you immediately!

My mission statement for my business is:

------------------------------------------------------------------------------

------------------------------------------------------------------------------

------------------------------------------------------------------------------

------------------------------------------------------------------------------

------------------------------------------------------------------------------

## ACTIVITY 3—

Using the bullet points in the business description and purpose section above, describe all about your business. If you have Estate Agency details of your chosen business premises, you might decide to include them in your appendix. Remember, if you are trying to secure money to set up your business, the more relevant information you provide your potential lender with, the more well- informed and prepared you will appear.

**Your business vision and long-term objectives.**

It is important to set a realistic view of the future for your business. If you give the impression that your business is all singing and all dancing, (either to your money lender or potential customers), you will send out mixed messages and may well deter the very people you are trying to attract. You need to be able to substantiate your claims and a sure way of doing this is to set yourself goals in the form of long-term objectives.

Anyone who has studied the principles of marketing will be quick to tell you that many products and services have a limited shelf life. The ability to remain market leaders and maintain a large share of their specific market as achieved by many companies and businesses, doesn't happen by chance. They will have kept a careful eye on market trends, what their competitors are offering and what they can offer that is unique or different.

Does your business have a Unique Selling Point (For example, the Nappy Network launched themselves as the only environmentally friendly nappy suppliers).
Do you have a specific niche market?
Is your business idea sound and well researched?
What do you see your business doing that no-one else is currently doing or offering?

# ACTIVITY 4—
# DESCRIBE WHAT WILL SET YOU APART
# FROM YOUR COMPETITORS

My business vision is:-

My USP is:-

## LONG~TERM OBJECTIVES

Not everything happens by chance in life and nothing could be truer when considering your long-term business goals.

You may find it easier to break your business goals down into short, medium & long term.

# ACTIVITY 5—
# IDENTIFY YOUR BUSINESS GOALS

As a starting point, list your most important short-term goals:-

Using the example of a 'soon to be opened' sandwich bar here are some simple examples:

- ✦ I will offer sandwiches, cakes and drinks to local passing trade

- ✦ I want to operate from 8.30-3pm five days a week

- ✦ I want my first 3 months turnover to be £5,000

My short term goals are:-

-----------------------------------------------------------------

-----------------------------------------------------------------

-----------------------------------------------------------------

-----------------------------------------------------------------

-----------------------------------------------------------------

-----------------------------------------------------------------

-----------------------------------------------------------------

-----------------------------------------------------------------

The sandwich bars medium-term goals might be:

- I will offer a sandwich delivery service to local shops and offices
- I will take on a part-time member of staff
- I will open on Saturdays from 8-2pm
- My turnover will increase by 25% within the first 6 months

My medium-term goals are:-

-------------------------------------------------------------

-------------------------------------------------------------

-------------------------------------------------------------

-------------------------------------------------------------

-------------------------------------------------------------

-------------------------------------------------------------

-------------------------------------------------------------

-------------------------------------------------------------

-------------------------------------------------------------

-------------------------------------------------------------

-------------------------------------------------------------

What about looking to the future? Where do you see your business in a year, two years or five years time?

The sandwich bars long term goals might be:

+ To open another sandwich bar in the 3$^{rd}$ year
+ To open another two in 5 years time
+ To ultimately offer a Sandwich bar franchise

My long-term aims are:-

---

---

---

---

---

---

---

---

## CURRENT MARKET SITUATION

This section covers information to show that you have researched your market as part of your planning & research. Again, you will have already given this some thought when working through STEP 3 on Marketing.

You can show your understanding of the current market situation by including details of your competitors, both locally and regionally or nationally. Is your business aiming to offer something different from your main competitors? Will it be attracting the lower or upper end of the market? If you do not know the answer to these questions, do some research online into demographics, (ie: looking the characteristics of a population regarding such factors as spending, income, population, socio-economic groups and migration) for the area you are going to base your business in. If you are going to be operating an online business, such market research can also give you an insight into trends within your chosen market.

(Try sites such as www.neighbourhoodstatistics.gov.uk & www.demographicsonline.com).

By doing careful research into your chosen business area, you will be better prepared to evaluate what is likely to work and what will not. This can be the difference between making your venture a success or a failure. It will also show your lender that you have done your homework and have made realistic decisions based on the information you have gathered.

For example, the prospective sandwich shop owner could visit other sandwich providers in the trading area and compare packaging, the range of sandwiches they offer and other items they sell, as well as their prices. A questionnaire could be drawn up to ask friends, family and work colleagues what sandwiches they prefer and why, where they choose to buy their sandwiches from and why and how much they are prepared to pay for their sandwiches.

Talk to and question as many appropriate people as you can, in order to make informed decisions, rather than guesses, as to what will work and what will not.

# ACTIVITY 6 –
# DESCRIBE YOUR CURRENT MARKET SITUATION

Having done some appropriate research, explain the existing market. You can include any research findings as an appendix.

Current market situation:-

------------------------------------------------------------

------------------------------------------------------------

------------------------------------------------------------

------------------------------------------------------------

------------------------------------------------------------

------------------------------------------------------------

------------------------------------------------------------

------------------------------------------------------------

You will no doubt have heard the expression, 'we must move with the times in our business' and in spite of the impact of the recent economic downturn, some companies will have failed to take into account changing market trends and external influences.

It is therefore very important to re-assess where your business is heading, on a regular basis, and to decide whether changes need to be made.

What would the likely impact on your business be of a

new ring road being built near your street? Is there any new legislation which is likely to impact on your business? (For example, when the new Disability Act was passed in the late 1990's, many thousands of businesses had to spend money on adapting their premises and toilets to accommodate wheelchair access in order to comply with the new legislation).

## Your target audience or customers

For you to successfully offer what it is your prospective customers want, it is most important that you can identify the profile of your expected customers.

For example, it would be pointless opening a luxury car sales showroom (such as Ferrari or Porsche) next door to a cut price supermarket or charity shop.

If you are offering a specialist product or service as opposed to something seen to be a necessity (a model railway shop versus a greengrocers, for example), the place you set up in, the products you offer and the price you charge will all be determined by what your targeted customers are able and willing to pay and how prepared they are to pay you a visit.

Ideally you will have a balanced portfolio of customers; your bread and butter customers and your more exclusive jam on top!

# ACTIVITY 7—
# MY TARGETED CUSTOMERS

Having completed some market research, (remembering to include any relevant findings as an appendix), consider the answers to the following points:

- Age
- Sex
- Occupation
- Spend per visit
- Customer profile
- Why will they buy from you and not a competitor
- What benefits are there for your customers in buying your products?
- Are your products & services seasonal or in continual demand?
- How will they pay? Cash/card, invoice, instalments, in advance?
- Other as appropriate to your business type

NB:-All of the above can have a large impact on sales, cash flow and profit forecast.

## EMPLOYEES

Whilst you may be the mainstay of the business and the only member of staff in the initial stages of starting your business, you may be need to employ someone to help you, even if only for a few hours a week while you buy stock, visit existing/potential customers or if you are ill.

Just as **YOU** represent your business, so will any staff you employ, and therefore it is vital that you choose people to work with you and for you that you can rely on and who will represent your business in an appropriate and favourable way.

Your business will become very much a part of you but it is a very fortunate business owner who can expect just the same passion and drive for your business as you have! Much will depend on how you treat your staff and what incentives and encouragement you give them but ultimately, making sure you know the type of person who would be ideally suited to working with you, will prepare you for when you need to consider taking on staff.

Once you have worked out your trading hours you will have more of an idea of the hours you need to be covered by another member of staff. You will also need to carefully consider what you can realistically afford to pay. Do you take on a young person with no experience you can train and pay the minimum wage, or will your business activities require a more experienced person and therefore cost you more?

Most firms will send out a job description with a job application pack as well as a person specification. Whereas the former describes what the job entails, the latter describes the ideal candidate the firm is looking for.

Here is an example of a person specification for a part-time sandwich bar assistant:-

| Essential qualities | Desirable qualities |
| --- | --- |
| • Good personal hygiene and appearance | • has previous catering experience |
| • Trustworthy | • can work a till and handle money |
| • Good time keeper | |
| • Excellent health | |
| • Has a basic food hygiene certificate | |
| • Good social skills | |
| • Can work flexible hours | |
| • Reliable | |

# ACTIVITY 8—
## STAFF PROFILE(S)

Taking care to comply with relevant legislation (STEP 6 looks at legal requirements), compile an outline or person specification.

| Essential qualities | Desirable qualities |
|---|---|
|  |  |

## Marketing Plan

**STEP 3** looked at some of the key marketing activities you need to consider when setting up your own business. Therefore you will be well equipped to include all appropriate and relevant marketing information as it applies to your proposed business.

# ACTIVITY 9—
# MARKETING PLAN

Use the information you have included in the seven activities in STEP 3 to illustrate what marketing strategies you have put into place in order to develop your business successfully. Not only will it illustrate to your lender that you have carefully considered a variety of marketing activities, it will also make you commit to taking action!

Remember, marketing is an ongoing activity so if you have ideas for the future as to how you could develop your business, do include these in the marketing section of your business plan, together with explanations of what marketing activities you propose to undertake.

# STEP 5 ACTION POINTS

◊ **Activity 1**—introduction

◊ **Activity 2**—write a mission statement

◊ **Activity 3**—business description and purpose

◊ **Activity 4**—your USP

◊ **Activity 5**—identify your business goals (short, medium & long-term)

◊ **Activity 6**—describe your current market situation

◊ **Activity 7**—describe your targeted customers

◊ **Activity 8**—design your staff profile (if applicable)

◊ **Activity 9**—compile a marketing plan based on STEP 3

# STEP 6
## Rules And Regulations---
## understanding and complying
## with all things legal

*'The minute you read something you can't understand,*
*you can almost be sure that it was drawn up by a lawyer.'*

**Will Rogers**

Anyone who owns or occupies a business premises or works for themselves, needs to understand the legal implications and obligations that affect them.

If you are buying an empty shop instead of an existing business, you may need to apply for planning permission and equally, if you trade from a Listed Building, there are certain restrictions you will need to be aware of. If you lease a building rather than buying it, there will be a legal obligation to comply with the terms of the lease.

There are Health & Safety, Building and Fire Regulations to be followed. Even how a business disposes of its waste can be governed by legal conditions!

By law, businesses are required to provide Health & Safety information to their staff including providing a suitable working environment for their staff. (For example, adequate heating, lighting, washing & toilet facilities as well as a suitable rest area for eating & drinking during breaks).

As your shop will be providing a service to the general public, you will be obliged by Commercial Law to cater for disabled people (i.e. making the premises accessible to them). Also, under the Disability Act, the business must not discriminate against disabled people who use the services or against disabled people who apply for employment.

Together with all the above and aspects such as Fire safety and even applying for a license if you choose to play music (**PRS certificate required**) or supply alcohol for consumption on the premises (no matter how infrequently), the list of legal considerations can seem very daunting to the new business owner.

However, do not despair! If you do your homework and seek appropriate support and guidance, everything should and will fall into place.

STEP 6 serves to introduce you to some of the important legal aspects to consider when setting up a business for the first time. Compliance with appropriate legislation will very much depend on the type of business you are setting up.

There is plenty of free advice available and you are strongly recommended to seek help & professional direction from any one of the organisations listed in STEP 7.

## REGISTERING YOUR BUSINESS

As mentioned in **STEP 2,** you will need to decide whether you are setting up as a sole trader or a limited company. (If you decide to run your business as a company, you will need to issue shares & appoint directors. There are also a number of legal requirements).

If you intend to trade as a limited company, you are required to inform Companies House as soon as possible. As a sole trader, you will not need to notify Companies House or deal with any administrative or accounting requirements which **are** required of limited companies.

However, whether you will be operating as a sole trader or a limited company, you are required by law to register with HMRC as self-employed, even if you already complete a tax form.

# ACTIVITY 1

Research www.hmrc.gov.uk and www.companieshouse.gov.uk and note what information you need to provide in the light of your proposed trading structure.

## HEALTH AND SAFETY LEGISLATION~~

Health & safety legislation can seem daunting at first as it relates to many areas of protecting the employee and the employer in the workplace. Government agencies such as **The HSE—(Health & Safety Executive)** provide useful advice. You will need, for example, to undertake RISK assessments (an example is included in the HSE pack).

If you employ more than 5 staff, they will need to be notified of safety procedures in the workplace via a staff handbook and signs should be displayed to highlight any hazards and to direct people to emergency exits.

The location of the nearest First Aid facilities should also be clearly shown and all accidents which occur in the workplace must be recorded, in case of any injury claim against your business.

**(RIDDOR—Reporting of Injuries, diseases & Dangerous Occurrences)** Under Health & Safety law, employers and those in control of the premises must report specified workplace incidents.

Another legal consideration under Health & Safety is that all businesses must conduct a **Fire Risk** Assessment of its workplace and check it meets all the necessary fire safety standards. You will also need to have a Fire Certificate.

Therefore it is advisable to seek advice from your local Fire Safety Officer at your local Fire Station.

If you are planning to open a business serving food and drink, it is also recommended that you contact your local Environmental Health Officer who will inform you of what legislation you will need to comply with.

# ACTIVITY 2

Research relevant Health and Safety Legislation and list what considerations you need to implement for your business, in order to comply with current legislation.

## LEGAL CONSIDERATIONS WHEN SUPPLYING CONSUMER GOODS

All transactions between the buyer and seller are **contracts** with both sides having clearly defined responsibilities. A contract is a legally binding agreement between two parties. The responsibility of the consumer under the contract is to pay for the goods or services and the responsibilities of the seller are much more complex.

### Consumer Protection Act 1987

This law deals with three main aspects of consumer protection:

- ✦ Product liability—so that customers are protected from damage or injury caused by faulty goods

- ✦ Consumer safety-in relation to, for example, electrical appliances and domestic electrical goods

- ✦ Misleading pricing—it is illegal to mislead consumers about the price of any good, service or facility.

## Sale of Goods Act 1979

This legislation deals with the legal responsibilities of the seller of goods to ensure the goods match the description. For example, if you describe a pair of shoes for sale as being made of real leather but they are actually made of a synthetic material, you would be breaking the law. The law also states that goods must be 'fit for purpose' and of a 'merchantable quality.'

## Sale and Supply of Goods Act 1994

This law replaces the 'fit for purpose' and 'merchantable quality' above with 'satisfactory quality'.

## The Price Marking Order 2004

This piece of legislation covers products, (not services) and covers aspects such as:-

+ Clearly displaying prices and units of measurement (e.g. apples cost £1.50 per kilo)
+ Prices must be clear, identifiable and unambiguous
+ Guidelines on items for sale and window (and similar display) of goods

Exemptions for the law are detailed.

## Data Protection Act 1998

All businesses that keep any information on living and identifiable people, must comply with The Data Protection Act. The act applies to any computerised or manual records containing personal information about people. The

Information Commissioners Office will advise you of your responsibilities. (www.ico.gov.uk)

If you are running an online business you will need to comply with

**The Consumer Protection (distance selling) regulation 2000** & **The Electronic Commerce regulations 2002**

# ACTIVITY 3

It is important to have knowledge your responsibility in relation to your business and the rights of your customers. Identify what legal considerations you need to consider in relation to your particular business if you are selling goods or services.

## INSURANCE CONSIDERATIONS

As there is much to consider when insuring your business, it is **vital** you seek appropriate professional advice. Your local Business Link advisor will offer free advice or you could go to The Citizens Advice Bureau (**CAB**) or a solicitor who specialises in employment law.

The following indicates what Insurances you should consider:-

**Employer Liability Insurance**— This enables businesses to meet the cost of damages and legal fees for employees who are injured or made ill at work through the fault of the employer.

**Business premises and Contents Insurance** similar to household Insurance but may cost considerably more.

Pavlenka Small

**Specialist Insurance** (e.g. loss of cash, goods in transit)

**Loss of earnings Insurance** (e.g. if you lose income due to road works outside your premises which restricts customers ability to visit your business for a couple of weeks)

**National Insurance** (class One for employees, Class 2 for self-employed people).

## EMPLOYMENT LEGISLATION

If you are planning to employ any staff, even if only part-time, you will need to be absolutely clear what legal obligations you have as an employer.

As always, seek appropriate, professional advice; the following information,(which has been sourced in good faith and without prejudice), is designed to give you a basic outline of what legislation you will be expected to comply with. Unfortunately, being ignorant of any legislation as it might apply to you, your staff and your business is very unlikely to stand up in a court of law.

Broadly speaking, if you employ staff you will need to consider the following areas:-

+ contracts of employment
+ employee records required
+ disciplinary and grievance procedures
+ a health & safety policy (if employing more than five staff)
+ holiday entitlement
+ maternity/paternity entitlement

- wages—national insurance, PAYE, national minimum wage

- holiday and sick pay entitlement

- equal opportunities

- CRB checks (if you or any of your staff are going to be working with children and vulnerable adults)

All such considerations are bound by legislation which you are required to comply with.

However, although all of the above may seem daunting, it is important to remember that there are specialist organisations who are there to give you guidance, support and advice.

## Activity 4~
## Sources For Gaining Advice On Legal Matters.

If you are planning to employ staff in your business, identify details of where you will go for support.

| Organisation | Information Required | Date Contacted |
|---|---|---|
| e.g.: Department of Work and Pensions | Current Minimum Wage | |

**STEP 7** gives details of some organisations that can provide you with appropriate advice. You may have met someone at a networking event who is a specialist in employment law or maybe you can ask an established, similar business to yours for advice.

### Employing the services of professional experts

Finally, you will need to set up a business account and invest in the services of a reliable bookkeeper or accountant. Again, ask around if you are unsure where to go as personal recommendation can prove to be invaluable.

# STEP 6 ACTION POINTS

◊ Activity1 –identify the most appropriate trading structure for your business

◊ Activity2 –research health & safety implications to your business

◊ Activity3 –determine what legal considerations apply if your business will be selling goods or services

◊ Activity4 –If you plan to employ staff, decide who you will go to for guidance and support

# STEP 7
## Useful websites

**Key:**    1 Employment

2 Legal/taxation

3 Business planning

4 Finance/funding/grants

5 Marketing

6 Free advice

7 Inspiring stories/case studies

8 Young people setting up in business

9 Workshops/training

10 Other

| Organisation—www. | 1 | 2 | 3 | 4 | 5 | 6 | 7 | 8 | 9 | 10 |
|---|---|---|---|---|---|---|---|---|---|---|
| acas.gov.uk | ✓ | | | | | ✓ | | | | |
| articles.bplans.co.uk | | | ✓ | | | | | | | |
| bgateway.com | ✓ | ✓ | | ✓ | ✓ | ✓ | ✓ | | | |
| bookevents.org | | | | | | ✓ | | | | |
| bplans.co.uk | | | ✓ | | | | | | | |
| businesslink.gov.uk | ✓ | ✓ | ✓ | ✓ | ✓ | ✓ | | ✓ | ✓ | |
| bytestart.co.uk | ✓ | ✓ | ✓ | ✓ | ✓ | ✓ | ✓ | | | |
| careers.ed.ac.uk | | | | | | | | ✓ | ✓ | |
| chas.gov.uk | | ✓ | | | | | | | | |
| cipd.co.uk | ✓ | ✓ | | | | ✓ | | | ✓ | |
| companieshouse.gov.uk | | | | | | | | | | ✓ |
| connexions-direct.com | | | | | | | | ✓ | | |
| croner.co.uk | | ✓ | | | | | | | | |

| Organisation—www. | 1 | 2 | 3 | 4 | 5 | 6 | 7 | 8 | 9 | 10 |
|---|---|---|---|---|---|---|---|---|---|---|
| direct.gov.uk | ✓ | ✓ | | | | | | | | |
| dwp.gov.uk | | | | | | | | | | |
| fsa.gov.uk | | | | ✓ | | | | | | |
| growingbusiness.co.uk | ✓ | ✓ | | | ✓ | | | | | |
| hmrc.gov.uk | ✓ | ✓ | | | | ✓ | | | | |
| hse.gov.uk | ✓ | ✓ | | | | | | | | |
| invent.org.uk | | | | | | | | | | ✓ |
| knowledge.hsbc.co.uk | ✓ | ✓ | ✓ | ✓ | ✓ | ✓ | | | | |
| lloydstsb.com/support/ business guides | | ✓ | ✓ | | ✓ | ✓ | | | | |
| menta.org.uk | | ✓ | ✓ | | ✓ | ✓ | | | ✓ | ✓ |
| mplans.com | | | ✓ | | ✓ | ✓ | | | | |
| princestrust.org.uk | | | | ✓ | | ✓ | | ✓ | ✓ | |
| prospects.ac.uk | | | | | | ✓ | ✓ | ✓ | | |

| Organisation—www. | 1 | 2 | 3 | 4 | 5 | 6 | 7 | 8 | 9 | 10 |
|---|---|---|---|---|---|---|---|---|---|---|
| shell-livewire.org | | ✓ | ✓ | ✓ | ✓ | ✓ | | ✓ | | |
| smallbusiness.co.uk | | | | | | | | | | |
| smarta.com | ✓ | ✓ | ✓ | ✓ | ✓ | ✓ | ✓ | ✓ | | |
| springwise.com | | | | | | ✓ | ✓ | ✓ | | ✓ |
| start.biz | | ✓ | | | | | | | | ✓ |
| startups.co.uk | ✓ | ✓ | ✓ | ✓ | ✓ | ✓ | ✓ | ✓ | | |
| successfulmarketing.co.uk | | | | | ✓ | | | | | |
| teneric.co.uk | | | ✓ | ✓ | ✓ | ✓ | | | | |
| topenterprise.co.uk | | | | | | ✓ | ✓ | | | |
| traintogain.gov.uk | | | | | ✓ | | ✓ | | ✓ | |
| uk-plc.net | | ✓ | ✓ | ✓ | | ✓ | | | | |
| ypla.gov.uk | | ✓ | | | | | | ✓ | ✓ | |

# FINAL STEP...
## Believe in yourself and go for it!

You have now considered and planned for all the key aspects of setting up your own business. So, you need to take the plunge and just do it.

If you don't believe in yourself and your own abilities, no-one else will and you wouldn't have the confidence to get started on what could be the best experience of your life!

# CASE STUDY 1

## MICHELLE STEER—RESEARCHER, WRITER AND EDITOR:

**Specialising In Working For And With The Caring Profession.**

'I set up my business as a freelance researcher, writer and editor four years ago and having had previous experience of working for charities and the caring profession, I decided to specialise in this area.

As a mother of a six year old, running my own business from home gives me the flexibility to choose the days and times I want to work with, no boss to answer to and also, no rush hour traffic to combat every morning.

The key challenges or negative aspects I have experienced is the effort needed to constantly market one's business (as well as understanding HOW to market oneself in the first place!), deciding how much to cost my time and how much to charge for my services. Also, not knowing what my income will be at the end of the year as well as the irregular nature of income on a monthly basis has been quite a revelation.

I would say the main thing I have learnt from being my own boss is that marketing is an essential and ongoing aspect of any business. It doesn't need to be expensive but it does need to be directed at the right audience.

**Advice I would give to those setting up a small business:**

Have a Business Plan that identifies what your product is and who your audience is going to be. A lot of time and money can be spent marketing your business to the wrong audience.

You also need to consider what you want to gain from your business: whether you want to earn a good salary, or for the business to work around your family commitments or to build and develop a large organisation.

Take every opportunity to attend free training courses; there are several available to small businesses and the self-employed.

**Michelle Steer**

# CASE STUDY 2

## CAROLINE GOULD—WEDDING PLANNER

I launched my business in 2009 having spent three years considering my business idea. Prior to this I worked as a hotel wedding planner but, as I was only ever involved in what happened at the hotel, I felt I could offer a lot more to the couples involved.

I took maternity leave in 2008 and spent the year I was off work researching how to run my own business and how to actually become a wedding planner. I did a course with The UK Alliance of Wedding Planners (www.ukawp.com) which really gave me a great starting point for running a wedding planning business. I also went on several Business Link courses (www.businesslink.gov.uk ) which gave me an insight into all aspects of running a small business. I spent the next six months writing my business plan and building my website before officially launching Endless Love at a wedding fayre in September 2009.

Being a self-employed business owner means I can set my own hours of work to fit in around my family and although the nature of my business involves some weekend work, I always ensure I balance this with family time during the week. I really enjoy the flexibility to work from home and work when I want to.

Running your own business requires good organisation and self-motivation; if you don't feel like working, no-one is going to make you but equally, no-one is going to do the work for you when you are not there. There is also the danger of working all hours and it is likely you will be unable to switch off from thinking about your business on your days off. Getting a good work/life balance is important and I am fortunate that I have a really supportive family.

I have learnt an incredible amount over the past two years and continue to learn all the time. The skills I have developed lead me to believe I could run a business doing anything!

**My advice for anyone thinking of setting up their own small business:** is to spend time writing your business plan and to keep an open mind. You will face many personal and business challenges in your first year of trading so, if you keep an open mind and ask for appropriate help where needed, you will undoubtedly have a successful business.

**Caroline Gould**

**www.endless-love.co.uk**

# CASE STUDY 3

## <u>Anthea Gillgrass~Independent Mortgage and Protection Advisor</u>

I had worked for Lloyds TSB since 2004 but a combination of trying to juggle being a single mum with a stressful job and a less than supportive manager, forced me to resign and set up on my own as a sole trader in 2005.

I had originally joined the industry due to personal experience; I was in the process of divorcing my husband and wanted to buy him out so I needed financial advice. I found I didn't receive the help, advice and support I needed and just felt like 'another sales statistic.' With personal determination and support from ex-colleagues at the bank, I was determined to succeed in setting up my own business. I funded my business with savings together with the view that I had to and would succeed.

I devised a business plan and put things into action. Contacting estate agents and solicitors as potential clients was nerve-racking but perseverance paid off in the end.

Investing in appropriate licences and approvals was a costly exercise, without the assurance of earning any money as a result. I also had to find a suitable network to operate in, (all of whom offer different benefits at variable rates), rather than being directly answerable to the FSA. The first network I chose turned out not to be sound and viable and I lost money.

The key difficulties I encountered initially were finding suitable clients whilst juggling child-care as a single mum and competing with the 'big boys' in the industry, all of whom had a wealth of knowledge. It was also a lonely existence; I hadn't discovered the benefits of networking initially which I regret as it is not acceptable to 'cold call' in the industry.

However the support I had from loyal friends and colleagues was invaluable. In 2007 when the financial market collapsed I also moved to another area and it felt as if I was almost having to start all over again. However, what still drives me on a daily basis is the fact I can help individual clients to achieve what is most appropriate to their circumstances.

### My advice to those setting up a small business:

Ensure you understand the purpose of setting up and running your own business as things will get tough. Try to have some savings and learn from wisdom not experience. Finally, ask the right people for help and guidance.

**Anthea Gillgrass**

**www.trustfinancialsolutions.co.uk**

# CASE STUDY 4

## JACQUI STONEMAN—
## CHILDREN'S NURSERY SCHOOL OWNER

I set up a children's nursery school in 2003, which runs as a limited company, and, based on the success of my enterprise, (we have just received an outstanding grade at our recent Offsted Inspection), I also work as a freelance consultant to other local nursery schools.

Having no previous experience of the industry other than being a mother of two children, I quickly realised I needed to learn at lightening speed. I interviewed as many people as I could to understand the things they loved and hated about their work and what had been the best and worst nurseries they had worked for and the reasons why.

I contacted various government agencies, (who tend to offer free advice), I joined various forums and went along to every seminar that was free of charge.

From the outset my aim was to be careful with costs and I purposefully kept overheads as low as possible by applying for every grant I was entitled to and involving the help of trainees and volunteers from colleges.

Based on my experiences thus far I would advise any would-be business owner to 'just do it' and learn from every mistake made. You will undoubtedly make mistakes but you will never succeed if you don't try! Rather than having regrets it is surely better to say that you tried.

Finally, keep smiling and always seek appropriate help; people are always happy to give free advice!

**Jacqui Stoneman**

**Just Consulting Services
(Supporting SME's to be successful)**

# CASE STUDY 5

## FRANCES GRIFFITHS~HYPNOTHERAPIST

I started operating as a sole trader with my hypnotherapy practice in 2004.

Having previously worked as a self-employed garden designer and interior landscaper for eight years, I had some experience of self-employment but although I had always been fascinated by hypnotherapy, it was a completely new area of interest. I therefore attended as many business courses as possible on subjects such as marketing, finance and sales.

As I operate from home and clients come to me, my biggest expense was my initial training which I funded by working in an office.

The main difficulty I experienced was the whole domain of marketing myself and my practice; not being a naturally demonstrative person I found it hard to 'sell' myself. Being self-employed can and will take you out of your comfort zone and you will find yourself doing things you didn't realise you were capable of. It is also important not to get despondent when things do not go according to plan.

I would recommend that any prospective business owner research what courses and help is available and to take full advantage of them. Also, as self-employment can be solitary, it is wise to make contact with like-minded people who can empathise with you and who will understand the particular issues which confront the small business owner.

**Frances Griffiths**

**www.harmonyinmind.co.uk**

# CASE STUDY 6

## MANDIE HOLGATE—BUSINESS COACH & OWNER OF THE BUSINESS WOMANS NETWORK.

I set up my two businesses in 2009, both of which enable me to empower, support and assist business women with their personal skills and confidence as well as giving guidance and encouragement with their businesses.

I currently operate as a sole trader and outsource several areas of my business. I was very excited at the prospect of setting up my own business; as a self-confessed workaholic, (and having previously worked long hours in the car trade), I was desperate to get back into a busy routine.

Ironically, my main concern initially was the area of sales and marketing as this was such a different area to my previous experience and yet I was recently nominated as a finalist in a local business award for Excellence in marketing. This allowed me to reflect on how much I have achieved in a relatively short period of time.

As a busy mum, it took a while to get the right work/life balance as well as learning to prioritise my business activities. My dad was an excellent role model and I listened to anyone and everyone for tips and advice about entering into the realms of self-employment. I discovered that 'so-called' experts are not always what they appear to be and took advice from my mum who taught me to 'take everything in like water into a sponge and wring out the useless stuff.'© This allows you to trust your instincts and separates the experts from the 'wanabees', without causing offence.

Guided by my parents business experience, I managed to fund my business totally from any earnings I made and I made sure I only ever spent half of what I earned.

My advice to anyone setting up a business is quite simply to 'go for it!' as well as undertaking thorough research, planning and getting to know your market. So many business women I work with have not put their heart and soul into making a full-time career out of their business and see it more as a hobby. This can be draining and demoralising. Before you do anything, develop your mission statement and identify what you want to achieve, why you want to run a business and what is important to you.

**Mandie Holgate**

**www.thebusinesswomansnetwork.co.uk**
**www.mandieholgate.co.uk**

# CASE STUDY 7

## BRIGETTE CURRIN—ELIZABETH VALDA ESTATES

In 2008 I decided I wanted to be my own boss. I returned to full-time work after being a full-time mum but I soon found I was missing out on important events in my children's schooling which I hated.

My main line of work had been within the administrative field so I set up my first business offering administrative services to small businesses on a freelance basis. I enjoyed being self-employed and wanted more of a challenge.

I met Christine through networking and we got on well right from the start. After a few months we knew we would work well together and decided to explore what options were available to us in order to run a business together.

At the time I was in the process of selling my house and was having little success, having engaged three local estate agents to sell our house and none of them seemed to offer an acceptable standard of service. We felt that by combining my administrative skills with Christine's 'Home Staging' expertise, we would be able to offer a personalised service unlike anything offered by existing estate agents.

We spent ten months planning, researching and training. I admit there were times I doubted we could do this as starting Elizabeth Valda Estates became a bigger venture than we had anticipated. However, we had invaluable help from our Business Link Advisor as well as gaining insight into the national and international world of estate agency via one of the UK's leading Estate Agency trainers.

The most important aspect of getting our business off the ground was to get our branding and marketing right. We found an excellent local firm who did an amazing job of hitting our branding right on the mark!

We also formed a brainstorming group with three other local business women and we meet monthly to support each other with any problems we might be encountering. This proved really useful when gaining constructive feedback on our website design and content.

Our business plan is something which is a continual work in progress; nothing is static in business and it is important to make necessary changes when required.

The hardest part of setting up in business has been to ensure I achieve the right balance between work and family life. Having a business partner has made it much easier than going it alone; it's great to have someone else's point of view and share ideas. However, it is essential you choose the right person to work with.

My advice to anyone starting out on business is:-

+ Write a business plan, set goals and have something to refer back to on a continual basis.

+ Find a Business Advisor who can guide you through potential pitfalls and helps you to think 'outside the box'.

+ Get your marketing right and develop sound branding.

+ Network regularly so that people get to know who you are.

+ Understand your cash flow and how you will be

making a profit. After all, that's why you are in business.

+ And finally, whatever your business is, give GREAT SERVICE.

**Brigette Currin & Christine Hamilton**

**www.evestates.co.uk**

# About The Author

Pavlenka Small considers herself most fortunate in that she knew what career she wanted to follow—to run her own restaurant—from a very early age. She passionately believes that everyone has the right to feel fulfilled, both in their personal and working lives.

With several years experience working her way up through the Hospitality Industry and gaining a degree in Hospitality Management, she opened the first Sandwich Bar in Peterborough in the mid 1980's and joined forces with her husband to fulfil their ambition of opening a restaurant in Lincolnshire together.

Having lost their business due to the recession of the late 1980's they went on to open and run a hotel in Essex and Pavlenka re-trained to become a hospitality and business lecturer at a local college, teaching 'would be' hoteliers and restaurateurs all aspects of the industry.

Having taken early retirement from lecturing in 2005, Pavlenka trained to become a life coach and now specialises in personal development and career coaching; supporting, guiding and challenging those who are particularly keen to set up their own business.

Pavlenka also works as a mentor with the SAM Project at CSV, guiding those with mental healthy issues back into the world of work.

She lives in the Suffolk countryside with her chef husband, Stephen and her son, Gideon, has provided the cartoons for this book.